THE LINEAGE
OF
KRIYA YOGA MASTERS

THE LINEAGE

OF

KRIYA YOGA MASTERS

Paramahamsa Prajnanananda

SAI TOWERS

PUBLISHING

THE LINEAGE OF KRIYA YOGA MASTERS

First Edition 2003
Published by
Prajna Publications
Diefenbachgasse 38/6, 1150 Vienna, Austria, Europe

Second Edition, 2007
Published by Sai Towers Publishing
Copyright © Prajnana Mission

Sai Towers Publishing
23/1142, VL Colony, Kadugodi, Bangalore 560 067, India
www.saitowers.com

A catalogue record for this book is available from the British Library.

Typeset in 10.5 point GoudyOIstBT

ISBN 81-7899-089-X

Printed in India by Vishruti Prints

DEDICATION

A flower blooms with beauty, purity, tenderness, fragrance and the sweet promise of honey that attracts the bees. A spiritual Master is like a flower in full bloom and each sincere seeker is a bee that comes to that flower in order to gain spiritual nourishment.

I came as a young bee to my Master, and he has both shaped and guided my life; whatever I am today I owe it all to him. With the foremost love and humility I offer my beloved Guruji and all of his Lineage this work on the auspicious occasion of his 93rd Birthday.

Prajnanananda

ACKNOWLEDGEMENT

No good work is accomplished without cooperative effort and
the blessings of God and Gurus. My sincere love and
appreciation to one and all who have helped me in various ways
to bring out this book.

God will bless them,

Prajnanananda

CONTENTS

The Kriya Yoga Origins and History

India has always been enriched and hallowed by a radiant constellation of mystifying and legendary great *yogis*, saints and sages well-known and revered for their highest spiritual upliftment and soul-culture. Since millennia, India has accepted renunciation and yoga as the *summum bonum* of human evolution. Many great *rishis*, saints and *kalpa-yogis* have attained the zenith, the ultimate apex, of God-realization and sown the seeds of soul culture. The soul elevating messages realized masters have preached, as well as their mesmerizing exemplary lives, have continued to shed unfailing awe-inspiring light on the true path towards the awareness of man's intrinsic divinity. In Indian mythology it is mentioned that even Rama and Krishna have practiced and taught the Kriya Yoga technique of meditation. It was explained by ancient *rishis* in the Upanishads, by Sage Vashistha and by Maharshi Patanjali in his *Yoga Sutras*. The Kriya Yoga Masters continue to inspire and influence *sadhaks* all over the world. Their exemplary lives are like burning lamps and as sacred as the scriptures; they cannot but rekindle divine impulses and impetus within the Kriya Yoga disciples, as well as in any seeker of Truth.

The ancient history of Kriya Yoga is mystifying and mesmerizing. Its origins are mysterious because they intermingle mythology, history and science in an extraordinary unique fashion and they go back to the dawn of consciousness.

In the beginning God alone existed, and He wished to become many. God projected the universe out of Himself, and with it His *maya* - the all-pervading delusive force of creation, but at the same time God also gave a supreme technique to overpower and overcome this *maya* by experiencing our own Divinity thus finishing the game or the treasure hunt He had started in the very beginning with His leela. This technique has been described in the Bhagavad Gita 9:2 as *"rajavidya rajaguhyam"* i.e. the royal science and royal secret technique.

In the Bhagavad Gita 4:1, it is said that God first revealed it to Vivashvan, Vivashvan passed it to his son Manu, the seventh of the fourteen Manus or progenitors of the human race - the Noah of Hindu mythology.

Manu then transmitted it to his son Ikshvaku, founder of the first dynasty of kings in ancient India. From then onwards this technique was transmitted from father to son, which metaphorically means from Master to disciple, through direct oral transmission. The Bhagavad Gita 4:2 even explains how this technique was then transmitted through a long line of *rajarshis* (royal seers), but due to the influence of the different cycles of humanity which bring about gradual degradation of spiritual values and an increasing fascination for material pursuits, this technique has been lost and rediscovered several times throughout the ages. It has always been God's promise that, at different critical times in human history, when dharma dramatically declines, He incarnates to restore the royal path that reunites man to the Divine. History records that Buddhism emerged and then almost disappeared, then Adi Shankara restored the original Hinduism and how Bhagavan Krishna, the great Avatar of God, incarnated at a certain point in time to rescue the lost righteousness and at the same time reintroduced this ancient yoga (Bhagavad Gita 4:3). Lord *Krishna* taught it to Arjuna and many other disciples, but with the inexorable passage of time, the royal secret technique was again lost.

In modern times, the history of Kriya Yoga starts in 1861 in a mountain cave in northern India, and continues until today, in India and in the West, through the grace and spiritual power of the lineage of Masters, the Kriya Yoga family, which is to say, the family of the whole human race.

Babaji

THE GREAT MAHAYOGI

Mahavatar Babaji Maharaj, the Master who brought back to the world the dynamic spiritual path of Kriya Yoga, is most mesmerizing and mysterious. Divine incarnations like Rama, Krishna, Mahavir, Buddha, Jesus, Shankara, Mohammed or Nanak have come and lived physically for a short time on this earth, while Babaji, being Mahakala, has conquered time and space and subdued death. Having realized his supreme essence and substance, Babaji has attained the greatest achievement ever possible: he is immortal, ageless and eternally young. Babaji is a great divine incarnation always engaged in the divine *leela* (play) of helping sincere seekers on the path of spirituality.

Nothing is known either about his birth, his family, spiritual training or his dwelling. No photographs of Babaji are available and the picture we are using in this book was drawn from the description Paramahamsa Yogananda gave after having seen him in his apparitions. Babaji's disciples know him by many names and address him as Mahamuni (the great Saint), Tryambaka Baba, Shiva Baba and Budua Baba (the ancient Baba). His miraculous appearances and disappearances have been narrated by his own direct or indirect disciples, outstanding spiritual personalities such as Lahiri Mahasaya, Swami Shriyukteshwar, Hamsa Swami Kevalananda, Brahmachari Keshavananda, Paramahamsa Pranavananda, Paramahamsa Yogananda and Paramahamsa Hariharananda.

Mahavatar Babaji Maharaj was the one who initiated Acharya Shankara, the spiritual reformer of ancient India and Kabir, the famous medieval poet, mystic and saint. The omniscient Mahayogi's physical form is a mere product of his own imagination and he has appeared in totally different forms even to the same devotee. Traveling astrally, he materializes a form to appear to his various devotees and continuously

1

changes his characteristics at will; therefore it is beyond human intellect to recognize him. Sometimes he has appeared as a *Bala-yogi* (child-yogi), a young handsome and glowing *Sannyasi* or as an astoundingly luminous Mahayogi with a long white beard and moustache. He has mostly been seen appearing in the area of Badrinath in the Himalayas and always surrounded by a group of spiritually highly evolved disciples or engrossed in deep meditation in solitary forests, remote caves or jumping from one Himalayan snow-covered peak to another.

Ignorance is the root cause of doubts, anxieties and duality. To bring down to earth his projected dream of saving humanity from the claws of unawareness of their inherent divine essence, in 1828 Babaji sent one of his advanced disciples back to the world. His soul took a new life and was embodied in a village of the Bengali Nadya district. This great soul was named Shyama Charan, (later on renown as Lahiri Mahasaya). This divine child was born to a *Brahmin* couple who was so devoted to Lord Shiva that, since the baby was only a few months old, his mother used to bring him along with her to pray and meditate in the family temple dedicated to Lord Shiva. The baby used to sit quietly, with his eyes closed, in a stillness similar to the state of deep meditation, his body would be covered with ashes just like *sadhus*, yogis or Himalayan saints and, it would often glow encircled by a radiant and suffused divine light.

One morning Babaji appeared in his awe inspiring luminous form at the door of the temple and said: "Mother, I am a *Sannyasi*, you have nothing to fear. Your child is not an ordinary child. I have ordained him to show a very simple path of self-realization both to householders and *sannyasins*. In future this child, while leading a normal family life, will be an ideal, respected and adored example of how even family men may lead a perfect spiritual life and attain enlightenment. He will show the way and lead many to the path of self-realization. I will be like a shadow following his form, protecting and guiding him. I will constantly keep an eye over him. Through this child my dream, my will, my *sankalpa*, will ultimately concretize and become a reality." Uttering these prophetic words, Babaji vanished.

Babaji had planned that Shyama Charan would study in the sacred pilgrimage center of Kashi (Varanasi) where he could enjoy the company of many advanced spiritual personalities. To give a final shape to his grand design, Babaji had him marry and find a job that would eventually transfer him in 1861 to Raniket in the Himalayas where Shyama Charan was to supervise the construction of a road and buildings for the army. One day, while Shyama Charan was transferring some office money escorted by armed policemen along a solitary mountain path, Babaji appeared out of thin air in front of him and, calling him by his name, said: "Shyama Charan! Why are you afraid? I knew you would come this way. I have been waiting for you for years and years. Tonight, after your office work is over, come and meet me again in this same place." Shyama Charan was bewildered and uncertain, but as Babaji's peerless, enchanting and divine glance had already pierced his heart, as soon as he finished his work; he went to the mysterious appointment feeling great waves of unswerving attraction in his heart. A divinely consecrated seed had been germinating during many births and it was now blossoming into its precoded divine plan, at the appropriate time and in the Himalayan perfect environment. Like a river speeding up before merging into the ocean, Shyama Charan quickened his steps breaking the silent stillness of the steep and dangerous ridges of the mountains. Out of the blue, he again heard Babaji's voice saying: "Come here, Shyama Charan!" As soon as Shyama Charan stood in front of Babaji, his mind and heart liquefied and he lost himself in his smile. The Sadguru and the disciple were reunited. Babaji's long wait had come to a close. Shyama Charan prostrated himself, entreating indirectly complete surrender at the guru's feet. After seconds of silent bewildering bliss, Babaji took Shyama Charan into a cave and asked him if he recognized the place, the tiger skin and the water bowl (kamandalu) that were in the cave. As Shyama Charan's mind was enshrouded by doubts and confusion, he shook his head and just underlined that he had to leave as next morning he would have had to be at his office. This time, instead of speaking in Hindi, Babaji amazed him by telling him in perfect English:

"You are not for office, office is for you." To uncover the veil of doubts of Shyama Charan's mind Babaji extended his hand and touched his disciple's head and with deepest compassion explained: "Shyama Charan, this is the play of Mahamaya. She has made you forget everything. In your past life you practiced meditation in this cave and this is the tiger skin and water bowl you were using. I have preserved them for you after you ended your life here. I have been beseechingly waiting for 34 years. Like a bird protecting its offspring under its wings, I have been watching over you since the day I appeared to your mother in the family temple." At the Master's touch, a divine electromagnetic current flowed throughout Shyama Charan's body and the entire universe disappeared from his mind. Gradually his past life as an ascetic surfaced in his mind. Overjoyed and in bliss, Shyama Charan finally acknowledged the eternal and sacred relationship that had always bound him to his Gurudev, Babaji.

Babaji instructed Shyama Charan on the need of a dip in the nearby river in order to purify his body and mind before he could initiate him into Kriya Yoga and that he also had to drink the oil he had materialized. In the nearby river Shyama Charan went through kaleidoscopic experiences and ripples of joy gushed from his heart. For several hours he was in divine ecstasy at the blessing of the reunion with his Guru. That night, at around midnight, one of Babaji's disciples came to call him and brought him to a stunningly magnificent palace effulgent with light. The disciple explained that in a past life he had desired to enjoy the majesties of a golden palace and on this occasion the Mahayogi had created that palace to exonerate him from his last bond of karma. Noticing Shyama Charan's bewilderment the disciple added that nothing was impossible for the omnipotent master and that creation was only the projected thought of the Creator. He clarified that those masters who have the power to unravel the mystery of creation, can materialize and dematerialize whatever they wish. Yet the existence of the palace, created out of the cosmic dream of the great Master, was as ephemeral as that of the stars and planets, the whole universe and all beings animate or inanimate. This was one of the yogic leelas of the Sadguru and Deva Purusha Babaji Maharaj.

Babaji's disciple and Shyama Charan walked through ornate arches and jewel studded corridors into a series of lavishly decorated chambers that were filled with wafting fragrances till they finally reached a huge hall where there was a throne adorned with diamonds and precious gems. Babaji was sitting on the throne in his usual lotus posture and as soon as Shyama Charan reached and bowed at his feet, he said: "All your earthly desires are about to be extinguished. Awake, this is a divine moment. Now I will initiate you into the secret science of Kriya Yoga. By Babaji's touch the delusive layers of Maya, intellect, ego and mind instantly and forever disappeared, so that Shyama Charan could be anchored in the Ultimate, Absolute Cosmic Consciousness.

Just as Arjuna was the medium to teach humankind the Gita, Lahiri Mahasaya's spiritual transformation was the means towards humanity's emancipation. The secret technique that up to that day had only been confined to sages and saints who were living in seclusion in the caves and dense forests of the Himalayas, had been handed over to the one who had the mission to spread this knowledge to earnest spiritual *sadhaks*. Just like a caterpillar turning into a butterfly or an iron rod into gold at the contact of a touchstone, a huge spiritual metamorphosis took place in Shyama Charan through the divine touch of the Sad Guru. He was transformed into a Mahayogi, a Yogavatar.

As soon as the sacred ceremony ended, Babaji instructed the assembled disciples to close their eyes. The palace disappeared back into the thought essence that had created it, proving once again the limitless power of great spiritual Masters who can create and dismantle universe-like-structures in and out of their cosmic dream. Babaji offered Shyama Charan an empty earthen vessel to satisfy his hunger and in a few seconds it filled up with hot buttered luchis, curry and sweetmeats. Though he ate with great appetite, his pot always remained full and, when he asked for some water, he discovered in total amazement that the same pot was again empty and filled to the brim with fresh water.

The historic reunion of the gracious Guru and the disciple culminated in the heightened waves of *Brahmananda*, the complete merging of the river with the ocean. Babaji showered on Shyama Charan his divine power and Shyama Charan entered the deepest layer of God realization, the state of *nirvikalpa samadhi*. For seven days he was established in constant God-consciousness; there was complete reunion of *jiva* and Siva.

Babaji, though guaranteed that he would appear to him whenever he needed, instructed his reluctant devoted disciple to go back to the world and continue his worldly life. On the way back to Kashi Shyama Charan stopped at some friends' house and, as they were skeptical about saints and their powers, Shyama Charan locked himself up in the bedroom to meditate calling on his Gurudev to come and change their minds. Though it was not a proper request, Babaji satisfied his prayers and materialized in the house allowing the wonder-struck skepticals to take *padnamaskar* and receive his blessings.

One night Yogiraj Shyama Charan was conversing in his drawing room in Kashi with one of his disciples, Swami Pranavananda, when Babaji walked into the room in the guise of a simple Hindustani young man. He was clad in a simple white *dhoti*; his hair was long and his upper body completely naked. Shyama Charan, recognizing his Guru, bowed and offered him to sit with them. Swami Pranavananda, not realizing who he was, was shocked to see his own Guru bow at the feet of a simple *Sannyasi*, so he stood stiffly and aloof without paying homage to Babaji till Shyama Charan explained who he was and instructed him to bow at Babaji's feet. Pranavanandaji prostrated and also received the great blessing of a very long conversation with Babaji who eventually stated that Pranavanandaji would soon attain the ultimate goal. The supreme Master's words concretized shortly after his visit. Swami Pranavananda attained the stage of *nirvikalpa samadhi* and also the stage of being able to appear and disappear in more than one place at the same time.

Hamsa Swami Kevalananda, widely known as Yogacharya Shastri Mahasaya, was an advanced disciple of Lahiri Mahasaya. While he was living in seclusion near Badrinath in the Hmalayas, often had the blessing of being in Babaji's presence. He could witness many of Babaji's cosmic *leelas* while he was teaching to his highly spiritually-empowered group of disciples both from the East and the West. He recounts that Babaji always had a bamboo stick (*danda*) with him and that each time the timeless Master uttered the command -*dera danda utaho*- all the disciples would immediately disappear from his presence. It was under Babaji's guidance and directions that Shastri Mahasaya happened to be Mukundalal's (Yogananda's) Sanskrit tutor. It was by listening attentively to Shastri Mahasaya's discourses on the Gita, Kriya Yoga and *sadhana* that Yogananda started to be deeply attracted towards the Kriya Yoga technique. Even this was Babaji's interwoven design, a divine plan, preordained intervention.

Once Babaji and his disciples were sitting around a huge blazing fire in the deep and dense forest. In that deep silence, all eyes were fixed on his superb and blissful figure when Babaji seized a burning stick and struck with a roar the back of one of his disciples. All the disciples were in shock. Kevalananda and Shyama Charan were among them. Perturbed by the deep suffering of the disciple, Shyama Charan remarked: "Baba! How cruel!" Babaji explained that he had intervened reducing the effects of his karma. The disciple, due to the decree of his past karma, would have had to die burned to ashes, but Babaji had nullified his karma by merely burning his back with the stick. Touching the disciple's back with his healing hand, Babaji added: "By striking his body with a burning stick, I bestowed on him a new life."

In another occasion an American devotee who was so determined to be with Babaji that he spent five years searching the Himalayan mountains and deep forests seeking for the opportunity to have his vision and ask permission to be accepted as his disciple, finally arrived in front of Babaji. The devotee's face was lit with ineffable joy and tears were rolling down his cheeks. He prostrated at the great Master's feet saying: "My search is over. Now that I have found you I will not leave you. I implore you to accept me as your disciple. I wish to take refuge at your feet." But great and severe was Babaji's test. He remained silent, unmoved by his humble devotion and aspiration. The foreigner had to beg and implore him again, but as he received no answer he fearlessly declared: "If I am denied to remain at your feet as your disciple, I will die for you and in your name." Babaji remained aloof and did not show any consideration at all, yet he simply said in a stern voice: "If you desire to die, then do. There is no point in talking about it."At these words the American jumped from the cliff crushing his body on the rocks below. Ignoring the divine play behind the incident, all the disciples were horrified. They never thought their compassionate Master could be so hard and they all stared at Babaji's innocent and grave face. After a few minutes Babaji instructed them to go down and bring back the corpse. When the dead body was brought to his feet, Babaji knelt down and touched the devotee's dead body with his hand. The American devotee suddenly opened his eyes and humbly prostrated at Babaji's feet while he was explaining: "By this I have performed two works: the test of perseverance and the test on the disciple's depth of love. Further, as in his previous life he was not destined to be my disciple, by this resurrection I gave him a new life and the great opportunity he so much desires. He may now enjoy the quintessential experience of being my disciple. His determination, patient and ceaseless efforts made it possible."

Babaji has not only appeared to Lahiri Mahasaya, but also to many other disciples. His apparitions would always convey the inspiration to manifest his design of spreading the message of Kriya Yoga. Babaji endowed each of the disciples he appeared to with the final achievement in their *sadhana*. Priyanath Karar, one of the most outstanding disciples of Lahiri Mahasaya who would become world-revered as Shriyukteshwar, had never seen Babaji, but had learnt about his greatness and divinity through his Guru's words and experiences. During a great *kumbha mela* at Prayag, Priyanath was roaming amidst a crowd of saints and *sannyasins* when he heard someone calling him: "Swamiji, Swamiji!" As at that time he was still a householder and not a *sannyasi*, Priyanath did not even turn round and proceeded walking with his usual brisk steps. A *brahmachari* stepped out of a tent and informed him that a great Saint wanted to see him. Amazed Priyanath followed the *brahmachari* inside the tent and when Babaji also addressed him as Swamiji, Priyanath replied: "Maharaj, I am not a monk. Why are you addressing me as Swamiji?" At this remark Babaji stressed: "It does not matter. I will anyhow address you as a *Sannyasi*. Nobody has ever disobeyed me. Will you not obey me?" Babaji, with his gift to foresee the future, that day predicted that Priyanath would become a monk. Priyanath immediately realized to be in the holy presence of Babaji, his *param* Guru (his Guru's Guru) and overwhelmed with joy, he prostrated at Babaji's feet. In the course of the conversation that followed Babaji said: "Obeying your Guru's instructions you are writing a commentary on the Gita. Please undertake another task on my behalf. The West is longing to learn the Indian *Sanathana* Yoga. You have to write a book that will synthesize the synoptic essence of Indian metaphysics with that of the West. It is of most importance and need to reveal the basic intrinsic oneness and unity of Western and Eastern philosophy." As Babaji knew that Priyanath was not sure whether he would be able to accomplish such an important task, he reassured him with these words: "Whatever emanates from this mouth is bound to happen. My words will materialize as truth. Have no doubts and start working on the book. When it will be over, I shall pay you a visit. Lahiri Mahasaya's life on earth is nearing its end and I will continue to spread the Kriya Yoga technique both in India and in Western countries through you." These were the words predicting the turning point for Kriya Yoga and its main exponents.

Priyanath soon finished the task of comparing and synthesizing the true intrinsic metaphorical meaning of the Indian Scriptures and the Bible. This wonderful book is now worldly renown as The Holy Science. As promised, Babaji appeared again to Priyanath at the Raj Ghat on the river Ganga where, every morning, he used to go and take a bath. Priyanath was elated and to honour the Great Master he begged Babaji to please come to his house, but as Babaji answered: "We are people who relish the shelter of trees," Priyanath ran home to get some sweets and some fruit, but when he returned, there was no one to be seen under the tree, Babaji had disappeared leaving him totally dejected. After few days Priyanath went to Kashi to visit his Lahiri Mahasaya. While he was offering *pranams*, Lahiri Baba asked him if he had noticed Babaji standing at the main entrance door, but as Priyanath replied that he had not, Lahiri Baba touched him on his head so that he could see him. Priyanath was excited, but Babaji reproached him: "Priyanath, you have so much anger and conceit. That day you threw away all the fruits and sweets! I had promised to come and see you as soon as the book was finished. I have kept my word, so there was no reason to feel so upset. Meditate more." Tears came to Priyanath's eyes and he humbly prostrated at Babaji's feet. Soon after Babaji vanished.

When they had met at the *kumbha mela* Babaji had instructed Priyanath to spread Kriya Yoga to the West, but as he had expressed his inadequacy to do so, Babaji had stated: "Alright, I will send you the right people." Babaji first selected Yogananda and then Ravinarayan, our Gurudev Paramahamsa Hariharananda. Babaji brought them both in contact with Shriyukteshwar who transformed them through his fathomless wisdom, exemplary detachment and strict discipline.

When Yogananda was to leave for the United States he was haunted by the desire to verify if that was God's wish and plan for his life. He meditated and meditated for hours on end with the increasing desire to hear God's voice and see Babaji's form. When his meditation reached a zenith where he was on the verge of breaking down under the weight of his fathomless inner passion, he heard a nock on the door. When he opened the door Yoganandaji saw a young renunciate who entered his room without uttering a single word and the door closed automatically behind him. Yoganandaji blissfully bowed and Babaji pacified him and reassured him with these words: "Yogananda! Obey your Guru and go to America. Know this to be the command of God. You shall be protected. You are the one I have chosen to spread the message of Kriya Yoga in the West. I guarantee you that it will ultimately spread all over the world. Through man's transcendental perception of God, harmony and peace will be established among nations." Babaji vanished leaving Swami Yogananda in divine ecstasy and infinite gratitude.

Hoping to meet Babaji once more, when Yoganandaji returned to India in 1935, he went to Allahabad *kumbha mela,* but as he did not meet him, from Allahabad he went to Brindavan. Here he paid a visit to Swami Keshavananda who was one of Lahiri Mahasaya's advanced disciples. A few months before Keshavananda had been to Badrinath where he could enjoy the blessing of Babaji's company. During one of their conversations Babaji had given him a message for Yoganandaji: "This time Yogananda will come to the *kumbha mela* hoping to meet me, but I will not be there. Tell him that I will meet him when the need arises." Hearing that Babaji had thought of him, Yogananda's heart started beating very fast and he felt overwhelmed with inexpressible bliss and love.

In 1949, *brahmachari* Rabinarayan (Hariharanandaji) experienced the bliss of direct contact with the great Mahayogi while he was then residing at Puri in Karar Ashram. That day he was meditating in his room having made sure that the door had been properly locked and bolted. All of a sudden the room unusually lit up. Though Rabinarayan saw Babaji's glowing form, he did not recognize him at once, but simply wondered how someone could have come in the room with a bolted door. Babaji was wearing his hair long, had broad shoulders and beautiful long eyes. On that occasion he was wearing a cloth round his forehead. After blessing Ravinarayan, Babaji disappeared. Still wonder-struck Ravinarayan started wondering if it could have been Babaji. At the thought of having missed such an opportunity and blessing, he desperately started crying and praying to Babaji Maharaj. Moved by Ravinarayan's anguish and devotion, Babaji reappeared in the bolted room. This time Ravinarayan could blissfully bow at his feet and receive his blessings fully aware of the Mahavatar's presence. Babaji inquired: "Why are you so impatient? I am satisfied with your *sadhana.* I always keep an eye over you. Through you my work will be completed." Then, looking at a basket full of fruit, Babaji asked: "If I taste this fruit meant for God, will you offer it to God again?" Ravinarayan instantly replied without indecision or doubt: "Why not? For me there is no difference between Shri Guru and God." Babaji accepted a fruit and vanished after blessing him again. When Ravinarayan asked the inmates of Karar ashram if they had noticed any Saint in the ashram, they all answered they had seen no one.

Ravinarayan was initiated into Sannyas in 1959 and became Swami Hariharananda Giri. In 1960, cherishing the desire to see Babaji again Hariharanandaji went to Raniket, but while he was walking on a lonely path, he heard Babaji's voice saying: "Hariharananda, why have you taken so much trouble to come up here? I will only appear before you out of my own will and in your Guru's hermitage. I am ever satisfied with you. You will successfully flood the Western countries with the streams of Kriya Yoga. Go back to Puri. You will not have my vision here." Hariharanandaji returned to Puri as the words of the Guru are the root of mantras, spent the rest of his life, up to his *mahasamadhi* on 3rd December 2002, spreading Kriya Yoga in Europe and in America.

All those who live in the Himalayas know about Babaji's manifestations and great *yogic* powers. When in crisis or adversity, they take refuge in Babaji. Some local people also invite him in their homes and offer Babaji and his group of disciples some simple food. One day a very rich man invited Babaji and his disciples for a grand feast, a *bhandara*. He also invited many other saints and sages from nearby localities. He wished to show off, to be envied and admired by his neighbours as his ego and self-conceit had no limit. The house servants worked for days on end to prepare the most beautiful and sumptuous banquet as the owner of the house wished that that occasion may be remembered by one and all as the greatest luxurious event in the local district.. That day Babaji decided to give him a lesson and arrived ahead of time. After a while Babaji expressed that he was very hungry and, though normally he only ate vegetarian food and could stay days and months without ever eating, that evening he behaved exactly the contrary and devoured all what was available in the house. Not only did he finish what was served, but also all that was kept in the host store rooms. All were astonished at Babaji's insatiable hunger. After finishing all that was in the house Babaji said: "Isn't there anything else?" The rich man fell at Babaji's feet begging forgiveness. When all the other saints and sages arrived there was no food at all left and the host would have been deeply humiliated in front of everybody. Having repented, Babaji saved him from the terrible humiliation and miraculously arranged sufficient food for one and all.

Babaji, the Supreme Yogi, brings fulfillment, gratification and perfection in all his most advanced disciples' lives, both in India and abroad. He is beyond knowledge; his cosmic *leelas* are beyond human intellect. *Mukti, kala* and *siddhi* (liberation, time and powers) are under his feet. His perfect divine plan has been woven and carried out in these past centuries and it still unfolds. His mythical yogic powers and miraculous achievements will shine forever in the hearts of his devotees, disciples and also in the awe inspired memory of the Himalayan villagers.

DIVINE TEACHINGS OF BABAJI

It is not proper to unnecessarily mention the name of the guru. By this, he is belittled.

One should leave the place where the guru is maligned.

The door of Kriya Yoga is open only to earnest seekers and sadhakas.

Shyama Charan, look! All this is the play of mahamaya, she is deluding you.

Be fearless.

I have been waiting for you for years.

The worldly man wants to realize God while continuing his daily life. But problems will arise for him, time is short. A simple, easy, unostentatious and highly effective Kriya Yoga is to be taught to them.

To renounce the world is not easy. Wherever man is, the world clings to him.

At present, the worldly man is helpless to achieve God-realization.

The sages and saints, clad with the bark of a tree, their eyes sunk in, their skin shrunk over their bony frame and their hair matted in locks, are the living idols of God as they move from door to door for alms.

Among the living, man is the best creation. He chooses one of two paths: A life as a householder or a life of renunciation. Where can be found the justification for creating differences between a householder and a sannyasi?

I always keep my disciples under my guard.

To serve a saint is sacred and brings great spiritual gain.

God is in every living body.

A living being means Shiva.

Patience, ceaseless efforts and strong determination make everything possible.

Lahiri Mahasaya

YOUR LIFE IS MY MESSAGE

"Your Life is my message" is the teaching of a great Master who silently taught his disciples the secrets of Kriya Yoga spiritual practice, and lived up to its ideal following Babaji's footprints. The Great Master Lahiri Mahasaya, up to the end of his life, carried on Babaji's instructions and mission. He was a true, devoted and sincere disciple of the mythical Master and also his brilliant reflection. Lahiri Mahasaya's advanced disciples used to say: "Who can fathom our fathomless Guru?" Even Shriyukteshwar often marveled at the wisdom which he unknowingly gained by simply sitting at his great Guru's feet while listening to what seemed to be simple, humorous talks. Though Lahiri Mahasaya never personally authored any books, his knowledge, his yogic and metaphysical interpretations of the Bhagavad Gita and words of wisdom inspired many of his disciples to write volumes about his interpretations of the Scriptures and his metaphorical teachings. Often the language, idioms and expressions of this realized Guru seemed beyond comprehension and, given the depth of his knowledge, an attempt to capture their essence is fraught with the possibility of misinterpretation. In the words of Swami Satyananda, endeavoring to evaluate our infinite Yogiraj would be as absurd as a salt statue trying to fathom the depth of the sea. Since his teachings were so complex, it becomes an uphill task to confine his spiritual expressions to worldly-sense-bound limits.

All along his earthly life Shri Lahiri Mahasaya transformed the existence of thousands of disciples through his exemplary character, divine wisdom, humble behaviour and love. His life was his teaching. His activities were gospels of truth and his life an ideal example. Shri Lahiri Mahasaya's life became the example of how one should lead a true spiritual life while living in the world as a fully responsible family man, erasing the common pre-concept that spiritual life is only the monopoly of a few celibates. He exemplified and taught that spiritual life was not a myth; anyone, from wherever one was socially or age wise positioned in life, could lead a life based on spiritual principles being constantly aware of God's presence in every aspect of life

EARLY TRAINING

He was born on Tuesday, the 30th of September 1828, in the small village of Ghurni, in the district of Nadia in Bengal. Like good healthy corn grows on fertile soil, *siddha-yogis* are born to very religious, spiritual families. The day of his birth was the seventh day of Durga *puja* during the Dasahara festival. The Lahiri family belonged to the ancestry of Vedic *Brahmin* Maharshi Bhattanarayan of Kanyakubja who had recently settled in Bengal. Lahiri's grandfather was a close friend of the then king of Krishnanagar, Raghu Ram Ray. As a token of his friendship, the king gave him the lease of Ghurani, which gave the family a good revenue and high status in society. Shyama Charan's father, Gourmohan, was a renowned pundit, a scholar of the king's court, well versed in the Scriptures and he had already gone up many steps towards self-realization. His first wife had expired in 1818 and he married Muktakeshi Devi whose devotion was so profound that she would not even partake of a drop of water before her morning worship was over. Lahiri grew up under the divine care of his virtuous mother and, as the influence and impact of the parents' example is very powerful on the moldable, pure mind of a child, Lahiri started to pray and meditate from a very young age.

One day Lahiri's mother, in order to finish her daily *puja* to the family deity, Lord Siva, left Shyama Charan on a sand heap outside the temple. When she remembered that she had left him all alone for quite a long time, she rushed out of the temple. To her surprise she found him smeared with dust all over his body, just like a yogi, sitting meditating with his eyes closed, irresponsive to her tentative to attract his attention. That day Muktakeshi realized that her child was no ordinary one. Out of the blue, while looking at her baby, she caught a glimpse of her revered Maheshevara, but could not really grasp the inherent reality of such a vision, as for a mother's heart her own baby always remains a child and nothing more.

When Lahiri was only five, his mother died and, as death often enables man to probe deeply into the meaning of life, underlining and evidentiating spiritual truths, he suddenly became more introvert and his conduct, demeanor and activities, at times, became rather strange and inexplicable. At such a young age, his mother's death was an eye-opener and Lahiri could perceive how dependent man was on the will of God, on the cosmic play.

Shyama Charan combined Gourmohan's scholarship, intellect and foresight with Muktakeshi's love, devotion and disciplined spiritual practice. He was humble, calm, quiet, serious and totally detached. As a boy he was very sweet, unconcerned about normal ordinary childhood games, he was almost always grave, dispassionate and introverted. A leader among his friends, Lahiri was never too concerned about his dress and would often go about in torn clothes. In his ingrained detachment and dispassion he would be content with whatever food was available. As a boy, and later as a young man, Lahiri Mahasaya was physically and mentally strong. He regularly practiced yoga *asanas* and meditated daily. He loved swimming and even during monsoons he would go and swim in the river Ganga. As from his early childhood spiritual practices had been ingrained in his spirit and routine, Lahiri Mahasaya led a healthy self-disciplined life. Like a silent and fearless warrior he always remained on the path of truth, always determined in his efforts as only a determined mind is able to perceive and realize the absolute truth.

After his mother's premature death in 1833, Lahiri Mahasaya and his father went to live in Varanasi (Benares), one of India's holiest cities on the banks of the river Ganga. Gourmohan's intelligence, mastery of Scriptures, scholarly erudition and, above all his engrossment in yoga, brought him great recognition among the scholars in Kashi. He took every step to make sure his son would receive good education according to the *Brahmin* family customs and, at his father's direction, he learned Sanskrit, Hindi, Urdu and Parsi. When the king of Kashi established an English medium school, he also learnt English and French and studied Indian and Western literature and philosophy. While he was studying the Vedas, the Upanishads and many other Sacred Scriptures, he always searched for new meanings and insights and, from his childhood onwards, Lahiri astonished everyone with his erudition and original interpretation of the Holy Texts. Later on in life, he mesmerized scholars with his explanations and profound analysis based on his own realization of the Scriptures' essence rather than the pure etymological one.

KASHIMANI DEVI

Shri Lahiri Mahasaya, after completing his formal education, in 1846, married Kashimani Devi who was the daughter of his father's best friend. Kashimani was an ideal life-partner. She was never idle and always got up very early in the morning. Further to serving faithfully her husband, her daily routine consisted of regular prayer and worship and all her household work. She was very religious and kind-hearted. She would perceive God in all the downtrodden and strived to help them according to her capacity. As women in those days never had the opportunity of a proper scholastic education, Shyama Charan, whenever he was free, used to teach his wife how to read and write. Thanks to the help and the support of her loving husband, Kashimani learnt to read and understand the Scriptures by herself, without the help of others.

In family life, husband and wife should really try to complement each other, they should help each other to evolve and grow. Marriage is not meant for the satisfaction of lower instincts to obtain sense gratification, but for leading a self-disciplined, regulated, moral life; to understand and encourage each other to attain the highest objective of human life. Marriage should not lead to quarrels or frictions; on the contrary, it should lead to understanding each other more deeply and to helping each other recognize both limitations and weaknesses. In family life most people become passionately attached to their wife, their children and their wealth, but Shri Lahiri Mahasaya always remained compassionately detached. Shyama Charan faced many crisis, difficulties and conflicts in his family and worldly life and faced them with sense of inner detachment and therefore emerged victorious. Problems are like fire; they serve to purify seekers' lives, making them inwardly strong. Many religious books and teachers declare that *kamini* (women) and *kanchana* (wealth) are the two great obstacles in spiritual life. Ignorant of the deeper meaning of this statement, many are quick to condemn and criticize women and wealth. But it is attachment itself that is the problem; attachment to anything or to any person is the main obstacle. Attachment is bondage.

Lahiri Mahasaya, having completed his formal education, started working in an office. However, his meager salary was not sufficient to maintain his family. So, in his spare time he also gave private lessons to some students in order to fulfill his family's material needs. Lahiri Mahasaya never had much money, but he was rich in his heart. He was always generous and kind. His charitable activities never stopped in spite of financial stress and strain. Shri Lahiri Mahasaya never complained about anything and in his daily activities always maintained a state of perfect equanimity.

SPIRITUAL THIRST

Lahiri Mahasaya's spiritual thirst kept burning stronger and stronger. His regular prayer, meditation and study of Scriptures were not enough to satisfy his unquenchable desire for self-realization. As he lived in Kashi (Benares), he could enjoy the holy company of many saints, sages and divine personalities, yet he was constantly longing to meet his own true Master who could help him speeding up his spiritual journey. In spiritual training, the role of a Guru is extremely important. Just as a baby learns how to speak from his parents and when he grows up and goes to school, he learns listening to his teachers.

Education, be it material or spiritual, always requires a teacher, a guide, a preceptor, or a guru who is well-versed and experienced in this specific subject. In addition to the practical side of his teaching, also the teacher's moral and ethical life makes a deep impact on the disciple's mind, as an exemplary character, an idealistic behaviour, profound insight and expression of love are the only tools to encourage and deeply inspire the students. Under the direct guidance of a guru a sincere disciple will feel that his life is being totally transformed. To find such a guide is a great blessing and a grand achievement in life. People search for mentors. They long to find the preceptor of their choice, but instead of searching for a guru, one should try to become a fit disciple. A disciple is one who is humble and ready to discipline himself at the feet of the master. Through sincere prayer and preparation one will definitely find his own predestined true Guru.

This is exactly what happened in the life of Lahiri Mahasaya. He did not dynamically seek out a guru. In December 1861 the divine guru drew Shri Lahiri Mahasaya to himself in the lap of the Himalayas. This meeting with his Master, as described in the previous chapter, although seemingly miraculous, was really pre-planned and pre-ordained. Lahiri Mahasaya himself, through his *sadhana* had obtained the divine grace of his great guru, Babaji. The meeting between Babaji and his worthy disciple brought the dawn of a new spiritual age. When Shri Lahiri Mahasaya was initiated into the tradition of Kriya Yoga, he received a foretaste of the inner spiritual journey that would eventually allow him to merge into eternity and the infinite. After his initiation Lahiri expressed his desire to remain with his guru, but Babaji sent him back to the world as he wanted him to be the example of how a perfect householder can carry out all his family responsibilities, but at the same time evolve spiritually. Lahiri Baba was instructed in all the ancient rules and techniques and on how to initiate others into Kriya Yoga, purifying the body, mind and past actions and on how a guru may transmit divine power to a disciple. Shyama Charan thanked his beloved Master with these words: "If it is an epitome of your grace to bring the Ganga stream of Kriya Yoga down to the earth, be kind to the worldly afflicted seekers by permitting me to initiate them into Kriya Yoga irrespective of caste, creed and religion." Shri Babaji mercifully granted his wish. When he returned to his working place he discovered that he had been absent from work for many days, but discovered on his desk a regular granted application for the exact period of his long absence. Shyama Charan mentally thanked his Master. All the enthralling experiences he had been graced with had totally rooted his immense love and devotion for his guru.

Householders often feel overwhelmed by their work and family responsibilities, but even the most legendary and renowned sages like Maharshi Vyasa, Sage Vasishtha, and Rajarshi Janaka, all reached the highest goal while leading a family life remaining inwardly and compassionately detached. Through spiritual practices men may learn how to control anger, ego and jealousy and cultivate divine qualities. From the rocky source of the mountain, the river flows down to give life to plants and animals. Similarly, spiritual life can find its supreme expression and perfection even in family and worldly life. Babaji Maharaj wanted to create a new spiritual ideal and order for the modern world through Lahiri Mahasaya who strove to fulfill the wishes of his beloved Guru. After this encounter Lahiri Mahasaya had and raised five children, two sons and three daughters, who eventually became spiritually highly developed.

From 1861 to 1885, Lahiri Mahasaya held office jobs and was dispatched to different locations in the Northern part of India, mostly in Kashi and Danapur. He was at the same time, a caring husband, an efficient parent and extremely reliable in his job. In 1851 he had joined as a clerk in a government military department. Notwithstanding all his duties and responsibilities, through his regular meditation, Lahiri attained all the peaks of spiritual evolution. He considered the night to be the best time for his meditation and, while all were sleeping, he was awake to enter into a deep state of meditation. He never imposed his ideas on his wife, but due to his loving and amiable nature, his wife was drawn more and more into spiritual life and took initiation into Kriya Yoga from her Saintly husband.

A miraculous incident happened during these years. It was Shivaratri and many pilgrims were flooding Kashi to have Lord Vishwanath's *darshan* and blessings. Kashimoni wished to go to the temple and, Shyam Charan obliged to make her happy. Once in the temple Kashimoni prostrated in front of Lord Vishwanath's image and when she looked up at Lord Vishwanath's statue, she saw her husband's face in the image of the Lord. Turning quickly to her husband who was sitting behind her in deep meditation, she saw him as the exact image of the Lord. She was flabbergasted and could not believe her eyes. That day the realization finally dawned that the man to whom she was married was none other than Siva incarnate. She kept this revelation secret and hidden deep in her heart, but from that day onwards, she never attempted again to keep Shyama Charan attached to worldly life.

Lahiri was very simple in his dress and in his manners. He always wore a *dhoti* and *punjabi*, the Indian traditional clothing and canvas shoes, but used wooden sandals while in the house and limited his needs to the minimum. He was at times very humorous and amusing, but throughout all his daily activities, he went on teaching deep spiritual truths. He never argued with anybody and though he never indulged in deep philosophical discourses or scriptural quotations, every one of his words was a scripture. Although he attained the highest state of spiritual realization, he always remained very humble. He was very loving and dear to all his disciples. Occasionally Lahiri, referring to the practice of Kriya Yoga, would say, "I have found a nice path. If anyone wants, I can tell them about that path."

In the Ashram of Panchaganga Ghat lived a Mahayogi, Tailanga Swami, who was considered as Lord Siva incarnated. He was a naked Swami and wore only a simple loin cloth. He had an exceptionally robust body and very long arms. He was endowed with extraordinary yogic powers and it was believed that he had lived in his physical form for over three hundred years. A disciple of Lahiri Baba once asked him to be accompanied to visit the naked Swami. Tailanga

Swami was giving a discourse to his devotees when they arrived at his ashram. As he saw Shyama Charan approaching, Tailanga Swami hurried to meet him and embraced him with extraordinary love. Tailanga Swami's disciples were astounded to behold such a gesture and such a profound respect between the two. It was the merging of two *maha-yogis*, one a stark naked renunciate, the other a white-clad humble householder, both self-realized souls ever absorbed in God. The disciples of Tailanga Swami, who did not know Lahiri Mahasaya, questioned their Guru about his guest. Swamiji replied: "What I and other Saints have achieved by renouncing the world and even a loin cloth, Shyama Charan has achieved still remaining a family man." Once recognized and praised by Tailanga Swami, Lahiri Baba's fame grew more than ever and he drew to the Kriya Yoga path many earnest seekers of self-realization.

Lahiri Mahasaya was the Guru and guide not only of householders but also of *brahmacharis* and *sannyasis*. He also accepted many *fakirs* (Muslim monks) and *derveshas* (Muslim mystics) as his disciples. While distributing his spiritual treasure he never made any religious discrimination and he always advised his disciples to be devoted, self-controlled and sincere in their practice and in the performance of good deeds.

One significant incident in Shri Lahiri Mahasaya's life will serve to illustrate his deep convictions. His second daughter had just died and they were waiting to take her to the cremation ground, her dead body had been laid in the adjacent room next to where Lahiri was teaching the Bhagavad-Gita. At a certain point they could hear a loud mourning from some members of his household. At this point, Panchanan Baba remarked, "Perhaps they are now taking the corpse away. Let us stop the discussion on the Bhagavad-Gita." Shri Lahiri Mahasaya replied with a serene smile, "They will do their work. Please continue yours". Upon hearing such a statement all the disciples were shocked and declared, "Our mind is not prepared to listen to the Gita at this time." The very next day, Rajachandra Sanyal, Shri

Lahiri Mahasaya's brother-in-law questioned him, "Please tell me, are you not affected by painful events such as the death of your own daughter?" The great yogi answered with a loving smile, "All may feel sorrow, but in the case of a person submerged in divine knowledge it is different. A small stone sticks to soft clay, but bounces off from a hard surface. Similarly, a painful incident cannot affect a person engrossed in meditation, it comes and goes. Only the ignorants suffer." Lahiri Baba always remained in the state of perfect balance. He was anchored in the state of *sthita prajna* and well-established in the state of divine wisdom.

When imparting initiation into Kriya Yoga, Shri Lahiri Mahasaya used to give the following advice to his new disciples:

You will not reveal the technique to anybody.
Consider women as the manifestation of the Divine
Mother.
As long as you are in the body, go on practicing Kriya.
When you are ill, practice mental Kriya
Try to be free from inner enemies such as passion, anger, and
so on.
Seek good company. Read the Bhagavad Gita daily.
Be humble at all times.

Every moment of his life was dedicated to the upliftment of man's spiritual awareness. His life was an epitome of the Scriptures and spiritual truth. Those who came in contact with him were elevated by his wisdom, love, and spiritual attainment. Lahiri Baba was part of Mahavatar Babaji's cosmic design. He propagated Kriya Yoga as directed and inspired by him. Day and night he was performing the divine task of bringing to light the hidden and forgotten Kriya Yoga technique, interpreting the Scriptures in the light of Yoga and attracting spiritually inclined people and Saints to the path of God realization and always had around him countless advanced disciples.

Swami Keshavananda was asked not to become a monk for many years by his Gurudev, Lahiri Baba, under the consideration that it would be 'sheer madness'. However, by dint of his *sadhana*, he eventually was allowed to become a monk. He lived in Brindavan and spent much of his time in the close company of Babaji Maharaj.

Asutosh Chattopadhyaya lost his father at an early age. Having and unquenchable thirst for knowledge, he was admitted to the Sanskrit College of Calcutta. With his genius, Asutosh succeeded in the examinations of law and literature and passed the Acharya and Shastri exams in Kashi and was granted the title of Vedanta Saraswati and became known as Shastri Saraswati. In his early youth he had come in contact with great souls like Shri Ramakrishna Paramahamsa, Mahatma Tailanga Swami and Bhaskarananda Swami. Not satisfied in his quest for a Guru, he kept searching until he found Lahiri Mahasaya. He received initiation and having also learnt *Vedanta Darsan* from Swami Bhaskarananda, under the spiritual guidance of Lahiri Baba Shastri Mahasaya, he attained perfection. His ten years of meditation in Kashi under the loving guidance of his Guru helped him attain the *samadhi* stage. He was Yogananda's Sanskrit teacher and when he accepted *sannyas* he became known as Hamsa Swami Kevalanandaji.

Among the equally advanced disciples who took initiation from Lahiri Baba is Swami Bhaskarananda, Shastri Mahasaya's teacher. He used to be engaged in deep meditation practices submerged in Ganga's icy waters during winters and lying on scorching sands in the full heat of the summer sun. Hearing about Lahiri Mahasaya's merits from his own student, he asked him to be introduced to Lahiri Baba and initiated into Kriya Yoga, yet requested that Lahiri Baba himself should have to come to his ashram. When Shastri Mahasaya referred this to Lahiri Baba, he disdainfully replied: "When you are thirsty, do you go to the well or does the well come to you?" However, through the merits of Shastri Mahasaya's meditation, the two great souls met in a garden in Kashi. Though highly revered among scholars, Swami Bhaskarananda immediately realized Lahiri Baba's infinite wisdom and with all humility received the Kriya Yoga initiation.

A neighbour, Chandra Mohan De, returned home after having obtained a degree in medical science. After having bowed to receive Lahiri Baba's blessings, Lahiri Mahasaya questioned him on various aspects of modern medical science and on how the physical body worked. Young Chandra Mohan was trying to explain with great enthusiasm, when Lahiri Baba asked him: "What is the definition of death?" Chandra Mohan started explaining from the perspective of his newly acquired medical knowledge. Lahiri Baba interrupted him asking to please check whether he was alive or dead. Chandra Mohan could not comprehend what he actually intended, yet out of curiosity examined Lahiri Baba's body. He could neither feel his pulse nor did the heart beat. There was no sign of inhalation, but his face was joyful and radiant. Bowled over, he re-examined the body, ineffectively searched again for his pulse and tried to detect his heart beats. He was flabbergasted and speechless. The new doctor prostrated at Lahiri Baba's feet totally baffled and confused. Lahiri Baba, with a beaming face told him: "Mohan, give me a death certificate." Chandra Mohan replied: "I can, but you are talking. A dead man cannot talk." The great Master told him: 'You must realize that there are still many things which modern science does not know of and cannot accomplish, while yogis can easily have access to such knowledge." This unique and direct experience erased Chandra Mohan's skepticism on the value of meditation practices and he humbly asked to be initiated.

Bupendra Nath Sanyal, one of Lahiri Mahasaya's most advanced disciples, received Kriya Yoga initiation in a dream. In 1893, when he arrived for the real initiation, he discovered that the initiation ceremony was an exact replica of what he had seen in the dream and that Lahiri Baba could exactly perceive what was in his mind. He rapidly progressed in his spiritual emancipation, in 1902 attained the state of self-realization and became an accomplished yogi. Known as Sanyal Mahasaya he became one of the pole stars of Kriya Yoga.

Shriyukteshwar's name, before he became a monk, was Priyanath. He had heard about the greatness of Lahiri Baba form some family friends who were his disciples. Priyanath found out Lahiri Baba's address and from Serampore went to Kashi. He gratified his life by seeing Siva incarnate as the Mahayogi, and instantly expressed his most humble ad fervent prayer to be initiated without any further delay. On 19th of August he took a dip in the sacred water of Ganga and wearing new clothes, he took initiation. He strictly followed his Guru's words and regularly practiced with love and devotion. He would often spend weeks at his Guru's residence discussing all his spiritual practice problems and listening to Lahiri Baba's interpretation of the Gita. His friend, Ram, also took initiation and both used to spend as much time as possible at the feet of their Guru. One day Ram fell dramatically sick. The doctors diagnosed Asiatic cholera and that his life was at a critical junction. Hearing this, Priyanath was in total distress and rushed to Lahiri Baba who coolly told him: "No need to worry." Consoled by his Guru's words Priyanath returned to the hospital, yet the doctors informed him they were helpless and could not save the patient's life. Priyanath started doubting his Guru's words. Grief stricken, while he was on the point of going back to his Guru's residence, he discovered that his best friend had breathed his last. In deep sorrow he went to his Gurudev. Lahiri Mahasaya, noticing his disciple had lost his poise and had tears in his eyes, simply instructed him to remain calm and meditate. Who can honestly meditate in such circumstances? Though Priyanath found it extremely hard, he obeyed and sat down to meditate. In the presence of the compassionate Master he went into deep meditation and remained in the *Samadhi* stage all night. Next morning Lahiri Baba gave him a bottle of neem oil instructing him to give seven drops to his friend Ram. Priyanath rushed to the hospital. When he went near his best friend, he saw that Ram's body was totally stiff and lifeless and all his relatives were crying around his death bed. Totally numb and notwithstanding the actual circumstances, Priyanath obeyed his Guru and gave Ram the seven drops of neem oil. When the seventh drop entered his mouth, his body started to shiver. Ram opened his eyes and amidst cries of stupefied joy, he got out of bed and started to walk. In baffled gratitude both friends immediately went to bow in total humility at their Guru's feet.

In 1894, during the *kumbha mela* Babaji had given indirect hints to Priyanath about the last scene of Lahiri Mahasaya's epoch. Babaji also gave similar hints to another disciple. Lahiri Baba unperturbed by life's events came to know about the imminent end of his life by the indications of his own all knowing Guru, Babaji.

One day, while Kashimoni was worshipping Lord Siva, Lahiri Baba appeared in front of her. She numbly stared at him in astonishment. In a very sweet voice her husband told her: "My work here is over and the time has come for my departure. I will be here only for another six months, then I will depart. Do not weep. You are the only one I am informing about my departure from the world. When this will happen, keep the body in my room for some time. After some time I will return. If I do not, then bury me in my room." Kashimoni did not pay much attention to these words. Lahiri Mahasaya fixed his date of death according to the position of the stars and planets and, a month or two before his death, gave hints about this also to some of his disciples. As the crucial day approached, he spent most of his days silently remaining in yogic postures, controlling breath and maintained a fixed gaze. Transcending all limits of body, mind and intellect he was constantly residing in cosmic consciousness, in the all-perfect fullness of Brahman. An end always has a means. One month before his death a boil appeared on his back. No treatment could heal it. Lahiri Mahasaya had himself cured so many ailments and fatal diseases by the application of his own preparation of neem oil, but even if that very same neem oil was applied, it was totally ineffective in this specific circumstance. In silence the great Mahayogi was peacefully waiting for his last day.

Some days before his *mahasamadhi*, Lahiri Baba was lying in bed. There was only his eldest son in the house who was keeping an eye on him from a distance. He was surprised to see his father stand up from his bed; walk around the room just like any healthy person, picked up a book from the book- shelves and then returned to his bed. His son slowly entered his father's bedroom and asked him: "Are you really sick? If you are healthy, why are you lying in bed all day?" Lahiri Baba smiled and commented: "Everybody has the deep desire to serve me, so I am lying in bed to fulfill their wishes."

On the eve of his *mahasamadhi* (final and voluntary departure from the physical form) Lahiri Mahasaya appeared in person before Swami Pranavananda, Swami Keshavananda and other disciples and gave them hints about his last journey.

On September 26th, 1895 Lahiri Mahasaya was lying in bed interpreting some verses of the Gita to his disciples. One of them asked: "What shall we do if you leave us? We will feel helpless. Do not make us orphans." Lahiri Baba pointed out: "Having obtained this great Kriya Yoga from Babaji Maharaj, I re-established it in this world. In future this meditation technique will spread to every house and man will gradually proceed towards ultimate realization. The secret path of realization shall ever remain open to mankind. The time has come for my departure. You should not weep. Even if this gross body is destroyed, the ever existent Guru is always with you." Having uttered these words he placed his head to the north. Being the day of Durga *puja*, drum beating and music was going on outside. In his deep meditative posture, remaining in *sahasrara*, Yogiraj Shri Lahiri Baba left his mortal body. Tears streamed from the eyes of his disciples and family members. Kashimoni had forgotten the hints Lahiri had given her some months before, so the disciples did not wait for some time before burying his body in his room and his body was immediately burned. It was the 26th of September, 1895.

From that day onwards, on both the auspicious dates of his birth and *mahasamadhi*, every *kriyavan* spends time in self-analysis and introspection pondering over Lahiri Mahasaya's message to transform their own life reflecting the truth of Kriya practice in their own daily life. After Lahiri Baba's *mahasamadhi*, his prominent disciples like Panchanan Bhattacharya, Swami Shriyukteshwar Giri, Paramahamsa

Pranavananda, Swami Kevalananda, Brahmachari Keshavananda, Sanyal Mahasaya, and both his divine sons Tinkori and Dukori Lahiri carried out the task of propagating Kriya Yoga to countless sincere seekers.

DIVINE TEACHINGS OF SHRI LAHIRI MAHASAYA

*Having learned this great and immortal yoga sadhana,
I re-established it with a wish that it will spread to each and every
house and that people will walk on the path to ultimate liberation.*

*The mind emanates from the soul. Good or bad are states of mind.
From the heart you must realize that sa is ham, which means the soul
and I are one.*

*Those who surrender everything to God while continuing on the path,
reap immediate dividends.*

Liberation is the ultimate goal to be achieved.

*The simmering flames of worldly life can be extinguished if someone
maintains his internal detachment while he is going about his
everyday duties.*

*Shun all thoughts about the past and future, do all your work with
your attention fixed on your breath (prana).*

There is no work without desire. Work which is duty bound is also born of some desire.

The world is a testing ground. Many examinations are to be taken. Man has to test himself. In all aspects of life, one has to be efficient and expert, so that no sense of wants remains. Do not allow your mental strength to weaken. Do all your work efficiently. Do not fear anything. Do not be deluded by satanic forces. Do not put your mind into anything other than the soul.

Those who remain merged in Brahman, worship Brahman and whether they are aware of it or not, they constantly realize the atom point within the kutastha.

Remaining ever in Brahman, above the head with full self-control one should stay still - in samadhi.

While perceiving Brahman, always try to have the conviction that "I am Brahman".

One whose words and mind remain secretly in Brahman is able to obtain everything.

If you want to know Him, enter into the body temple.

Our main duty is to still the mind. If the mind is not controlled, sadhana is flawed. If worldly duties are not properly performed, man looses his own humanity.

The mind is restless because prana (air) is always fluctuating. If the process of inhalation and exhalation is regulated and introverted by yoga, the mind also becomes introverted and still.

In Kriya, to remain in the super-conscious state of extreme tranquility or paravastha means liberation.

So long as man has not subdued his animal nature, he will not be able to discover the Divinity within him.

Do not be negligent in your duties.

By removing restlessness through sadhana, you will attain the stage of calmness.

We are all immortal souls, nobody is big or small.

If the mind is on kutastha, it is not sin, and if the mind is not on kutastha, it is sin.

For the practice of yoga three things are necessary: a healthy and strong body, undeviated determination and good will. Whoever has these treasures can practice yoga without impediments.

Since we are all God's children, we all have equal right to practice yoga for God-realization, irrespective of whether we are male or female.

The world is a propitious field for sadhana. You can obtain anything, even while living a worldly life.

Prana is both father and mother. Prana is son and friend as well.

Unless and until one humbles oneself, it is not possible to enter the spiritual realm.

Wisdom is above and beyond modern science; yogis have easily glimpsed into that wisdom where modern science cannot reach.

If one's will is set on God-realization, one can attain it even while living a worldly life.

The same soul exists in all living beings, due to this there is no obstacle in the way of soul culture.

Ephemeral love is not real love, eternal love is necessary.

By devotion and love to the guru, everything becomes possible.

Attachment is an obstacle. If there is no attachment, then there is no obstacle.

If the mind is not controlled and kept still in Brahman, knowledge of the Self (atma jnana) is impossible to attain.

It is not true that you do not have time for God-realization.

By practising Kriya in the morning, the vices of the night will evaporate and by practising Kriya in the evening, the sins of the day will be obliterated.

Without work nothing can be achieved and God cannot be realized.

Try hard, then you will get everything.

If the mind is always fixed on your guru and the soul on the name of 'Rama' (atma ram) you will hear the divine sound constantly and you will enjoy being in the secret chamber (chorakothari) which is filled with spiritual treasure. It is immensely good for you to remain quiet and motionless in that inner chamber.

Forget your past suffering and troubles. If you set your mind on self-realization and work towards your spiritual upliftment, you will receive immense benefits.

Keep doing everything with an eye on God and guru. Inherent in that is your good, since atma or your soul is your real guru.

If Kriya Yoga is practiced sincerely, all the negative instincts and emotions created by the senses and the mind like jealousy, greediness, attachment, pride and thinking ill of others will be subdued and instead you will enjoy divine, uplifting, euphoric sensations and loving impulses, which will gush out from within.

God is so close, but nobody seeks Him within.

Do not wait for guru kripa (guru's grace). If you practice according to your guru's instructions, his grace is automatically manifested.

When you go to the temple, do you bow down in front of the temple? You should bow down in front of God in the temple. Without God and Deity the temple has no value.

God lives in you. Instead of seeking Him in the distance, seek Him near and very much within you.

If you dive down deep into your heart,

you will perceive Him,
but, you will not by remaining outside.

In the internal sadhana, there is no need of external elements and
rituals. Only mind and prana are essential.

If one continues practising, communion with the soul is bound to
happen, whether one is ready or not.

While on a pilgrimage to a long and distant place, one comes across
many beautiful scenes and shrines.
If one stops in any specific place out of attachment to any of these
scenes, one will fail to reach and behold the final destination.

Remain fixed in nothingness.

Similarly while practising Kriya for self-realization, many gods and
deities will automatically appear before you. Do not stop there, you
have to keep going ahead. If you move ahead without interrupting
your voyage, these gods and deities will guarantee that you reach your
destination by extending their own helping hand.

If you do not know Brahman, you are mistaken.

You are filled with the whole limitless universe (brahmanda). Except
for you, nobody is the Lord of the universe.

Realization of one's Self (atma karma) is the real work to be
accomplished. Do not drown yourself in an ocean of activities
thinking that you are doing good to others. Whatever is being done is
ephemeral. To show the path to the rediscovery of the soul is the only
permanent good that can be done in the world.

If the mind is always entranced and engrossed in the Self, God will be found.

By being humble you can achieve greatness.

Never eat too much, take only what is easily digestible.

As long as you have not reached your destination, keep on practising Kriya and surrender your mind completely, leaving all doubts, mistakes and fears aside.

Before knowing God, know your own Self. Look inside your Self. Self-realization is God-realization.

Keep on doing Kriya! In the process of making, ultimately you will be made.

The guru is always conducting everything; he is always present as the kutastha. Guru is all pervading and permanently gracious. You are your own guru within your Self.

The sense of 'I' and 'mine' extended to any object causes moha (attachment). Attachment to an object frequently disturbs the mind. Always remember, everything belongs to God and nothing belongs to you. Always be in paravastha, while performing Kriya.

In every breath merge with the soul. Practice makes one perfect.

Do not waste time thinking about ephemeral things. Who can disown and avoid the effects of his past deeds? Your sole duty is to do your present work with attention fixed on prana, discarding all thoughts over past and future.

Swami Shriyukteshwar

GOD MADE ME A MONK

Swami Shriyukteshwar was an outstanding and unparalleled Master and quite different from any other Saint of the Kriya Yoga lineage. He was more introverted, less inclined to talk, and most of the time was absorbed in God-consciousness, deep in the *shambhavi* stage. Even when his eyes were open, he was constantly merged into infinity without any awareness of the outer world. He was so breathtakingly awe-inspiring that even his closest disciples were often a bit nervous to approach him and did not dare to talk openly and freely to him. Swami Shriyukteshwar was a realized Master and had an extremely authoritarian and strict personality. One day a disciple asked him a question with reverence and awe: "Swamiji, as you achieved the state of *nirvikalpa samadhi* while you were still leading a family life, why was it necessary for you to become a monk?" Shriyukteshwar answered with a smile, "God made me a monk." This was a very straightforward and simple answer revealing a great spiritual truth.

Shriyukteshwarji was born on the 10th of May 1855, at Serampore, on the banks of the river Ganga. His childhood name, Priyanath, means "the Loving Lord". From a young age he was highly spiritual and spent his life seeking a worthy spiritual guide. Born in an affluent aristocratic family he was naturally interested in literature and had good general knowledge. He was sharply intelligent and inquisitive and unquenchable fervor to know more and more led him to be successful in all his school exams and exceptionally brilliant both at college and medical school. He never studied to simply obtain a degree for a future profession that would allow him to earn his living, but studied science, physiology, anatomy and medical science in particular, to know more about the inner truth that lies behind human existence. Yet he never felt satisfied and always strived to learn more. Besides his regular studies, Priyanath studied in depth the Holy Bible and contemplating on its teachings, he could perceive the authentic hidden truths of Christianity and Jesus' teachings. Priyanath realized the essential similarity between Hinduism and Christianity.

Priyanath's main objective of those years' quest was to know the secret mystery of creation. Analyzing the connection of the individual soul with the universal spirit was the major goal of his life. He became interested in astronomy and cosmic astrology and their intrinsic practical applications. He was fascinated and curious about miracles attributed to saints and sages further to yogis' astonishing feats and achievements that science was far from being able to explain. Whenever he heard of such incidents, he would go and verify or to know more about this subject. He therefore came in contact with many saints, sages and masters since he was he was very young. He approached various different saints and sages, yet his thirst still was not assuaged. He met Tailanga Swami, Swami Bhaskarananda Saraswati and Guru Maharaj of the Radha Swami order in Agra. He did not hesitate to approach *tantriks* or *vaisnavas* to obtain their advice on spirituality and was loved and accepted by every teacher he came in contact with. In recognition of his knowledge he was admitted as a member of the Theosophical Society. So intense was his zeal to learn that once, hearing about a tribal saint, he went into the forest to meet him and expressed his desire to learn from him. The spiritual practice of this saint was the only one of its kind. Late at night on a full moon day he would dance and sing with his disciples. This was performed in secret and no one was allowed to witness this performance, but that night the Saint allowed Priyanath to attend the extraordinary and unique event. Many devotees gathered in the impenetrable forest under the silver rays of the full moon to dance and rejoice in ecstasy. Beholding this fascinating performance, Priyanath's heart was overflowing with blissful joy. On another occasion he hid under the bed of a saint who was renowned to levitate during his meditation practice, but due to his presence in the room, the saint could not concentrate and when he found out that Priyanath was hiding under his bed to spy him, he lovingly scolded him.

Priyanath used to say: "If one analyses the teachings of various saints with a devoted and open mind, one perceives the oneness of their teachings and one's sectarian frame of mind and ingrained pre-concepts dissolve."

After the death of his beloved father, Kshetranath, he inherited his father's business and land and became a very rich young man. At all times he loved and served his mother Kadambini Devi, a God-conscious and loving mother. When his mother asked him to get married, he fulfilled her wish and God's will without protesting and took up the household tasks and duties of a family man. He never neglected to love his wife, but his mind was always directed towards the ultimate truth. In course of time he was blessed with a daughter. Priyanath, although a man of sharp intellect and talent, was never particularly attracted by business. This resulted in financial loss and eventually his family business came to an end. He had to join an important business company as an accountant and although he had to earn his living paying attention to worldly duties, his mind was always fixed on his cherished desire of realizing God. As Priyanath was of the opinion that if one works under someone for a length of time he ultimately becomes his servant, after a few years he quit his job and was satisfied with the income of his ancestral property.

Priyanath studied homeopathy as he felt that it was the best among all types of treatments, but was also interested in naturopathy. Through his research and profound study, he was able to correlate the scriptural healing pattern with nature therapy. Not withstanding his family life, medical knowledge and study of astronomy and astrology, he still felt dissatisfied and unfulfilled. Priyanath did not remain caught in the noose of the illusory world for very long. After few years of family life, his wife passed away and his daughter got married. Soon after, even his only daughter died at a very young age. Throughout all these trials he remained impassively detached and looked upon them as *karmic* results from previous births. From that moment onwards he devoted all of his time, energy, skills and brainpower solely to the study of the Scriptures, astrology and practice of meditation.

Being omniscient, God knows the heart of a true seeker and when a disciple is ready, he helps him find a realized Master. When Priyanath was 28 his search for truth became more intense. There was no one left in the family except his old mother and he felt a great emptiness, all his interests in life had disappeared. At this life junction he came to know about the great Guru Yogiraj Shri Lahiri Mahasaya through some Serampore friends and relatives. His discriminative mind was immediately strongly fascinated by this mysterious *yogi* who was even inspiring and attracting him through his disciples of Serampore. He became very restless and as soon as he discovered that he lived in Kashi, he decided to go and meet him. Without delay Priyanath secretly left for Kashi. Not knowing the exact address, he relentlessly searched street after street till he found Lahiri Mahasaya's house. When he entered, he was awe-struck. The great yogi was sitting in *siddhasana* in deep meditation among many devotees. Priyanath felt a great elation and his heart filled with warm, joyful bliss. His questioning mind became very tranquil and meditative. Recognizing his Master of many past lifetimes, with infinite love and devotion Priyanath instantly humbly bowed in complete surrender. He felt the distance between disciple and Master disappear just like a tributary dashes to unite and merge in the main river. Here was the divine Master sent to guide him on his spiritual path. As it became late all disciples left except Priyanath who was sitting in a corner of the room. Priyanath slowly approached the Master and Lahiri Baba, at first glance, was aware of all his previous births and foreseeing his future, could assess his spiritual balance sheet. Yogiraj accepted Priyanath as his disciple and the time of initiation was fixed for the 19th of August 1883. Priyanath took a sacred dip in the River Ganga and wore new white clothes before approaching his Master for initiation. This day opened up a new chapter in the history of Kriya Yoga as the fountainhead of Kriya passed on the ancient technique to Priyanath. The worthy Master and the worthy disciple were being reunited in their divine mission of spreading the sacred Kriya Yoga technique. From that day onwards Priyanath sincerely devoted himself to meditation and Kriya practice and became Lahiri Baba's dearest (*priya*) disciple.

Priyanath constantly felt the living presence of his Master in his heart, in his soul and in every breath. He had accepted his Guru as his whole life. Having lost his father as a child, lost his wife in his youth, Guru became everything for him. Bestowed with many divine powers, Lahiri Mahasaya helped him with his own divine energy. Priyanath used to spend the majority of his time in his master's room and the holy company of his Master accelerated his spiritual development. Even while he was living in Kashi with his Master, he remained secluded, silently withdrawn and limited his talk with others to the minimum. When many disciples and devotees were present around the Master, he quietly sat in a far away corner of the room practicing *sambhavi mudra* and would approach Lahiri Baba only after all the devotees had left to seek his advice or show him some of his writings. Priyanath imbibed the taste of the divine nectar of scriptural interpretations from the lips of his beloved Master and as he had an excellent knowledge of Sanskrit, he was able to study the Scriptures in their original texts. Priyanath, by totally surrendering to the benevolence of his Master, progressed rapidly and ultimately ascended to the highest peak of realization constantly remaining absorbed in the uninterrupted state of divine bliss, *nirvikalpa samadhi*. In the Bhagavad Gita it is said that among thousands only a few yogis may sustain the necessary effort for God realization and even among these few, only the most fortunate attain the rarest state of perfection. (Bhagavad-Gita VII, verse 3) Blessed by Lord Vishwanath, he soon became the new leader to carry the flame of Kriya Yoga. Having always been a seeker of truth since his childhood Priyanath was conferred the title of Jnanavatara (Incarnation of divine wisdom.) While Shri Lahiri Baba, even if he was a family man, was destined by God to be a divine Master, a torchbearer of Kriya practice, God vision for Priyanath was to go all the different stages of being a householder yogi, a realized Master and eventually even a monk.

The Indian spiritual tradition and way of living, from time immemorial, is encapsulated in four *ashramas* or distinct stages in life:

1. *brahmacharya* – a life of self-discipline dedicated to education and meditation, while immersed in a state of perfect purity and celibacy;

2. *grihastha* – a householder's life, following all scriptural injunctions to lead a moral spiritual life;

3. *vanaprastha* – a life of inner detachment and selfless service;

4. *sannyasa* – the last stage of complete renunciation and spiritual life as a monk of the Swami order.

Priyanath successfully completed each stage of life with discipline and love for God and became a realized Master. Long before he decided to accept *Sannyas*, Priyanath had received the divine *darshan* and blessing of Shri Babaji, the divine and eternal Master of Kriya Yoga, who while blessing him, had addressed him as "Swamiji". From 1894 Allahabad *kumbha mela* onwards, everybody started calling him "Priyanath Swami" or "Karar Swami". After this meeting where Babaji had asked him to write a book where the Indian and Western philosophies and metaphysics were compared, his mind became suddenly inspired by Babaji's will and he immediately started the holy project of writing one of the most beautiful books, *The Holy Science*. About a decade after Babaji's blessings and the *mahasamadhi* of Shri Lahiri Baba he decided to accept *Sannyas* from Swami Krishnadayal Giri, a monk from Bodhgaya whom everyone loved, and came to be known as Swami Shriyukteshwar, which means "One who is always merged and united with God and His divine glory" and as a monk he raised even further in spiritual stature.

In 1895 Lahiri Baba left his body and the world. The pole star of the spiritual sky had vanished and his absence left a great chasm in the hearts of the devotees and disciples. Though he was not visible to the gross eye, the Master continued to guide his disciples in a subtle way. For years Priyanath continued to go to Kashi in the house where his Master used to live, but later on he turned his own ancestral residence, Priyadham into an ashram in Serampore. The interest and attendance to the ashram activities rapidly increased as Priyanath organized conferences to spread Philosophy, Astrology, Astronomy, Scriptural study, reading the Almanac etc.

The parents of Mukundalal (Yogananda) were direct disciples of Lahiri Mahasaya. When they took Mukundalal as a baby for the blessings of their Guru, Lahiri Baba predicted the future of the baby saying: "This baby, when he grows up, will enlighten the whole universe with his wisdom and will guide many spiritual aspirants on the path of Kriya Yoga." The words of both Babaji and Lahiri Mahasaya became true with the extraordinary meeting of Mukundalal and Swami Shriyukteshwar. As soon as they met Shriyukteshwarji's words resulted in divine vibrations in the mind and heart of young Mukundalal and the company of the Master made him experience bliss and ecstasy. Sometimes, out of the blue, Mukundalal's mind became numb and thought free and in that thoughtless stage, he realized that Swami Shriyukteshwar was a manifested embodiment of the Divine.

After a few days of his stay in the ashram, Shriyukteshwarji asked Mukundalal to return home, but as Mukundalal was reluctant to do so, Shriyukteshwarji firmly told him: "If you do not listen to me and return home, I will never accept you as a disciple. Now you go. Meet me in Serampore in a month time." Mukundalal halfheartedly left Kashi. Though he was traveling around India, in his heart he only longed to be with his Guru. When, after one month, he went to Serampore the great Master accepted him as his disciple, taking over all the responsibilities for his spiritual progress. Mukundalal managed to spend most of his time with his Guru in the ashram and practiced Kriya Yoga for long periods of time and with firm determination. Swami Shriyukteshwar taught him many hidden spiritual truths and took maximum care to ensure his spiritual growth. After completing his intermediate course in Calcutta, which was 40 kilometers away from Serampore, Mukundalal joined the Serampore College for his graduation courses in Bachelor of Arts. This gave him more time to be with his Gurudev. Although he was residing at the college hostel on the banks of the river Ganga, he remained at the ashram for almost all the time, which accounted for many absences at school. His intense desire and regular practice took him to new heights on the Kriya path, so notwithstanding all his absences, he could graduate simply by the grace of his Master. In 1915, after having obtained his degree of Bachelor of Arts from the University, Shriyukteshwarji formally initiated Mukundalal into *Sannyas*. Mukundalal became Swami Yogananda Giri and Serampore a place of pilgrimage for him as it was the land of his own spiritual transformation. In 1916 Yogananda had an opportunity to visit Japan by sea. He did not consult Shriyukteshwarji nor told him he was leaving. Though Swami Shriyukteshwar did not approve of this trip he personally went to bid him goodbye. In 1920 Yogananda left for America to attend a seminar of world religions as a representative from India. Blessed by the infinite compassion of his Master he affirmed the glory of India at the congress and after his talk, he remained in America and thousands took Kriya Yoga initiation. Shriyukteshwar often wrote to his disciple to return to his motherland, but with no success as Yogananda was very busy with many projects. After 15 years, in 1935, Shriyukteshwar sent this message: "You must come back to India with a return ticket at least for a few days, leaving your activities, however important they may be." This time Yogananda could not neglect the call of his Master. In August Swami Yogananda for the first and last time returned to India. Serampore witnessed the great reunion of the great Master and his worthy disciple. It seemed as if the two souls were merging into one. This reunion of the embodiment of wisdom and the embodiment of love was a day to be remembered in the history not only of Kriya Yoga but also of India. Swami Yogananda then left for Ranchi and came back to Serampore on the 22nd of December for the winter solstice celebration and next day Shriyukteshwar blessed his disciple declaring; "Today I declare you to be a Paramahamsa."

In early March 1936 when Shriyukteshwar came to know that Yoganandaji had gone to Prayag for the famous- Allahabad *kumbha mela*, his ashram inmates saw their Master in a depressed state. Some said: "We have never seen our beloved Gurudev in such a despondent state. The man of wisdom and lion-like courage seemed paralyzed by despair." Love and attachment can bind even realized souls, but Shriyukteshwarji soon recovered and attended a program in Bengal where, during a lecture he stated: "This is my last program." He went back to Puri and sent telegrams to Yoganandaji and Satyanandaji to come urgently to the Ashram. Satyanandaji was ill and Yoganandaji had other plans in Calcutta and postponed his departure by one day.

At the age of 81, in Puri Karar Ashram, on the 9th of March 1936, Shriyukteshwarji called his devoted Narayan who was always present near his Master and told him: "Narayan, it is time to depart from the world. Today I will leave the body." Sitting on a small bed in lotus posture Swami Shriyukteshwar asked Narayan to hold his chest with his two hands. Narayan followed his Master's instructions. The great Master and yogi went into deep meditation. His body was still when Narayan could feel a mild vibration pass through his heart up to fontanel producing a divine sound which resembled to the Om. As that sound merged into the cosmic sound, the great Master consciously left his gross body. Aboard the train, on his way to Puri, Paramahamsa Yogananda could intuitively feel that his Master might be no more. When he arrived in Puri he sadly prostrated at his Master's lifeless body and after bathing in the sea, he buried him in the northern corner of Karar Ashram.

The day after his death an old lady came to the ashram wanting to see him. When informed about his death she was very surprised and said: "but this morning I talked to him as he was passing by my house. How can this be?" Blessed is the divine mother who could witness his cosmic play.

On the 19th of June 1936 Paramahamsa Yogananda, before leaving India, was in a hotel room in Bombay. Yoganandaji was in deep meditation when he suddenly saw a glowing bright light. He opened his eyes and his beloved Shriyukteshwarji was there right in front of him. Yogananda, not having had the opportunity to be with his Master at the moment of his death, had been feeling rather sad. Sensing his disciple's feelings, Shriyukteshwarji told him: "Why are you unhappy? Am I not always with you! See I am with you even now!" Yoganandaji numbly stared at his Master. It was an unbelievable experience because he had in front of him his Master's same physical body that he had just buried in Karar Ashram. As if reading his mind Shriyukteshwarji said: "Yes I am your Master. I have come here in flesh and body and I am standing in front of you." Swami Yogananda has beautifully described in his famous book *Autobiography of a Yogi* the interesting description Shriyukteshwarji gives about his after death experiences and the lovely conversation that followed between the Master and the disciple.

Swami Satyananda, in Puri, had a similar experience. He had the privilege of receiving the divine touch of his Master's manifested form.

The youngest disciple of Shriyukteshwar was Rabindranath, who later on would be world renowned as Paramahamsa Hariharananda. Shriyukteshwar several times requested this young man to take charge of Karar Ashram, but young Rabindranath had not accepted the proposal as he was not yet mentally ready for it. In the beginning of June 1938 Rabindranath came to Puri. Before coming to Puri he had sent one of his friends to arrange for a rented house close to the Ashram. On a hot summer evening, Rabindranath and his friend were relaxing on the second floor balcony enjoying the cool breeze of the sea. Suddenly Rabindranath thought he had seen Shriyukteshwar walking from Karar Ashram towards the house and saw him passing by several times. At this he cried out: "Look my Master is coming!" His friend looked in the direction he was pointing at and became pale. When he recovered from the shock he explained that he had met the same person at the ashram when he was looking for a house for rent and he was the one who had given the information about that particular house. Rabindranath was exhilarated. Seeing his Master in physical form after his demise was for him an extraordinary event. After few months, having received directly from Shriyukteshwarji clear indications to join the Ashram, Rabindranath joined Karar Ashram as Brahmachari Rabinarayan. Thus Shriyukteshwar's desire was fulfilled. For many years the Shryukteshwarji's burial place remained under a thatched roof house. Brahmachari Rabinarayan meditated there for many years and received the blessings of his Master. He initiated into Sannyas by the Shankaracharya of Puri and has been spreading the message of Kriya all over the world just as Babaji had predicted. In 1971, after Swami Satyananda's demise, he was elected President of the Karar Ashram.

DIVINE TEACHINGS OF SWAMI SHRIYUKTESHWAR

Accept the ascetic life as a service to God.

*Do all work without deviating from the center of
self-knowledge or do all work centered in self-knowledge.*

Do service only for the purification of oneself.

*To be established in existence, awareness and bliss is of utmost
importance and all other work becomes secondary.*

*Pay attention to tapas, svadhyaya, and ishwara pranidhana in every
step of life.
(He emphasized the observance of these five points to his sannyas
disciples in order to become successful monks.)*

*The life of householders should be like that
of a river serving others.*

All judgement is determined by rajasic attributes.

Every householder should leave his house at least once a year and remain in seclusion for intense spiritual practice, either alone or under the direct guidance of a Master.

All work that man is capable of doing in this world, is still inferior to Kriya properly performed in unshaken knowledge and devotion.

Men of wisdom are neither deluded nor haunted by the spectre of birth and death. One should, without being inordinately confused by the words of wise men, follow strictly their methods of Kriya.

The endless, eternal Supreme Self lives equally in all, and never perishes with the body.

When one is completely rid of passion, anger and lust, which are the root of all desires, and the mind is controlled by the practice of Kriya — ascends to heavenly peace and tranquillity.

Every day do regular svadhyaya coupled with meditation and study of spiritual books and scriptures.

Those who shun all longings, lust and cravings, become devoid of any attachment, passion, ego or personal inclinations and are able to arrive at the stage of ultimate peace.

If the mind is made calm and quiet by the Kriya obtained from a satguru, the sun, the moon, the planets and stars can be experienced within the body. This stage cannot be ascended by sheer acquisition of indirect knowledge or induction, it is only possible by direct realization. Only by completely surrendering oneself at the feet of a satguru, can one ascend the heights to this kind of wisdom.

Dhyana (meditation), jnana (knowledge), tyaga (renunciation) and shanti (peace) are, respectively, like four stages of sadhana. Citta being pacified and controlled by meditation needs to be retained and anchored in divine enthralment by none other than wisdom.

Attainment of wisdom gives rise to the death of all desires. In this way, if one is established in meditation, wisdom and renunciation, citta becomes introverted in the sushumna, demonstrating always a peaceful disposition. Sushumna is none other than a haven for peace. When citta is turned calm and still, the eternal all-permeating chaitanya manifests itself.

The performance of duties with unflinching attachment is one of the fundamental reasons that cause worldly bondage. Even some intelligent people often hesitate to untie themselves from the fetters of this kind of attachment and remain imprisoned within their bodies.

If one performs one's duty perfectly, one derives happiness. The mind has a deep inclination for bliss and joy and an entrenched aversion to misery and suffering which are the consequences of unrighteous deeds.

If one purifies the mind with undeviated devotion and love one will perceive the all-pervading infinite chaitanya (consciousness) as an all-glowing sun within oneself. When one enters into such a state, one is able to see a luminous halo emanating from the soul center three inches deep from the middle of the eyebrows, right at the opening mouth of sushumna. This luminosity spreads to all centers in the sushumna and runs through the nervous system to encompass all body parts, illuminating the body with its glittering brilliance.

Imagination is the very negation of wisdom and it becomes the source of all suffering. Through imagination one is deluded into conceiving

what is transient as eternal, suffering as happiness and matter as soul. Chaitanya (chidabhas) is the manifestation of the Creator of the universe and thus becomes the inner light of a being. Without this guiding light from within the being does not perceive or see anything. It is the consciousness of your inner Self that gives you the power of seeing. The seen and the seer are intrinsic parts of your indwelling soul.

In every place, once a week, there should be a spiritual congregation or satsanga.

All roads to ultimate liberation are closed, whether one's work is righteous or unrighteous, unless one's sense of body, mind, intellect and ego completely withers away and dies in the infinite essence.

First of all understand the nature of man. Then, try to unearth the purpose for which man descended on earth. Without a deep awareness of the nature of the universe, any attempt at understanding the causes and purpose of the universe will be fruitless. If one follows the path of truth, one can easily understand the hidden meaning of the Gita, the Bible or any other holy scripture.

We can find the whole universe reflected in the human body. The more the sadhakas advance in their ultimate voyage to God-realization, the more they realize the veracity and profundity of tattwas of the universe indwelling in their own bodies through the science of yoga.

Like removing one nail with the help of another nail, the evil propensities can be weeded out by good samskaras.

For the propagation and proliferation of one's ideal and sadhana, you should form small spiritual groups.

Every day practice meditation, recite spiritual songs, discuss these among yourselves and render service to each other.

To lead an ascetic life is not child's play. To become a saint is not a religious show nor does it entail the exhibition of miracles, it is only for God-realization.

If man does not remain absorbed in God, his downfall is imminent.

In creation everything is governed by a rule. In the external world scientists have discovered rules governing nature. But underneath, hidden very deeply and subtly inside are the rules and canons of the entire universe; the manifested representation of Brahman. By doing yoga and meditation you are able to realize this.

Control of senses by Karma Yoga or Kriya Yoga is preferable to indifference towards the senses.

If man becomes judicious, reasonable and attentive about everyday ordinary things, he can go on to achieve higher goals.

Wisdom is not a mere exhibition of one's dexterity in giving a lecture. The average scholar studies Philosophy superficially and searches only the outward meaning. In this light University degrees and honours seem inferior and are almost trivial. True darshan (philosophy) means self-realization.

According to Kriya Yoga one will surely reach the ultimate goal if one keeps one's inspiration fixed on the ideal and one's attention completely absorbed in the soul.

Meticulously, the righteous and guru-blessed sadhakas, while discussing philosophy, understand the hidden meaning of the Gita and other Holy Scriptures, then, also by practicing the eternal happiness-promoting asanas and pranayama, the fickleness and doubts of the body and the mind will tend to disappear.

If, through practice, one always trains the mind to stay absorbed in the sushumna, then through this royal path, the divine energy will flow; as a result life becomes calm and quiet.

Shri Sanyal Mahasaya

THE RADIANT YOGI

As a young boy of sixteen, he stood in front of his future great Master with a handful of flowers, praying to be accepted as his disciple and to be initiated into the holy path of Kriya Yoga. Although the boy had already been initiated in a dream, he wanted confirmation and to learn the technique of Kriya Yoga more accurately. The divine guru, looking at the purity and humility of the boy and realizing his future with his divine insight, decided to be his guide on the path of self-realization. This happened on the 23rd of June 1893, in Benares, in the holy abode of Shri Lahiri Mahasaya. The young boy was Shri Bhupendranath Sanyal, who later became a *Yogacharya*, a teacher in the Kriya Yoga order of the Lineage of Shri Babaji Maharaj and Shri Lahiri Mahasaya. Shri Bhupendranath Sanyal is also popularly referred to as Sanyal Mahasaya.

THE HOLY BIRTHPLACE OF SAINTS

Shri Sanyal Mahasaya was born on the 20th of January 1877, in a hamlet called Sadhan Para in the district of Nadia, Bengal, on the East coast of India. Nadia is considered one of the holiest places in India, because in this area many divine personalities were born. Sons of Nadia include Shri Chaitanya Mahaprabhu, a great incarnation and devout follower of Shri Krishna in the 15th century, Shri Krittibash Ojha, the author of many Holy Scriptures in Bengali including the translation of the great epic the Mahabharata, and Shri Lahiri Mahasaya. In a later period also, Shri Sitarama Das Omkarnath, a well-known Master of the 20th century, was born there. Sri Sitarama was a *vaishnava* saint and was also the cousin of our beloved Master Paramahamsa Hariharananda.

At the age of two, Shri Sanyal Mahasaya had lost his mother, so most of his childhood was spent with his maternal uncle, his elder sister and her husband, who nurtured him and took special care of his education. Like a flower, he grew and bloomed with inner joy and spirit. He was always truthful and honest, sincere and divine. Due to his good behaviour and stainless character, his friends as well as his teachers always appreciated him, inspired him to excel in whatever he did.

From his childhood, Sanyal Mahasaya was spiritual, he never wasted time unnecessarily and he spent his leisure time reading the Holy Scriptures. Having been born into a brahmin family, he grew up in an excellent spiritual environment. His sacred thread ceremony was performed in 1890, when he was thirteen. At the same time, he was initiated into the *gayatri mantra*, which he practiced sincerely from that moment onwards. As he was growing up he was fortunate to enjoy the company of many saints, monks, and spiritual personalities and he also visited many holy places. Good company makes one good. The Spiritual environment and the good company he kept created in him the desire to lead a disciplined, spiritual life.

In his childhood, he was often sick and suffered from many ailments. At times his health conditions would become so serious that there was almost no hope for his survival. Due to his frequent illnesses, he was unable to take the different exams in school and later on, in college, but inspite of this, he never neglected his studies and spiritual practice.

In 1893, he was initiated into Kriya Yoga, but after only a short time with his Master, he had to go back to school. He lived in a student's hostel where it was not possible to practice Kriya regularly due to the presence of his school-mates. However, "where there is a will, there is a way". When all the other students were sleeping, at midnight, Sanyal Mahasaya practiced Kriya. His friends and room-mates never knew about his meditation and Kriya practice.

During this period, Sanyal Mahasaya fell very sick. After appraising his condition, his sister wrote to Lahiri Mahasaya about his meditation and sickness. She felt anxious for her brother. In reply, Shri Lahiri Mahasaya wrote; "He will not leave his body now, nothing will happen. He has many things to do". Sanyal Mahasaya's sister was consoled. The omniscient guru knows the destiny of his disciples. Later on in life, Sanyal Mahasaya enjoyed good health and vitality.

From 1893 to 1895, Shri Sanyal Mahasaya was several times blessed with the holy company of his guru. With deep devotion and love, with humility and surrender, he followed each word and instruction of his Master. Additionally, he maintained regular correspondence with Shri Lahiri Mahasaya. In this short period, he progressed rapidly in his Kriya practice. Although Sanyal Mahasaya was very young, Shri Lahiri Mahasaya allowed him to teach Kriya and he is alleged to have been the youngest *acharya* in the Kriya Yoga tradition.

Shri Lahiri Mahasaya, who knew the past, present, and future, was aware of his own impending departure from this material world, so he wrote to Shri Sanyal Mahasaya, instructing him to learn all other higher techniques of Kriya practice from one of his advanced disciples, Shri Panchanan Bhattacharya, the founder of the Arya Mission Institution, and then to go on to spread the teachings of Kriya Yoga to sincere seekers. On the 26th of September 1895, Shri Lahiri Mahasaya entered into *mahasamadhi*, the final exit from the body.

A LIFE OF ACCOMPLISHMENTS

Shri Sanyal Mahasaya completed his college education but was not able to continue his studies due to a change in family circumstances. He felt a strong desire to become a monk, but that wish did not materialize either as his destiny was to be a householder yogi, following the footprints of his Master. In 1898, at the age of 21, he married Kali Dasi Devi, a devout and pious lady. His spiritual practice never foundered in spite of his marriage and diverse family problems.

In 1902, Shri Sanyal Mahasaya reached the state of self-realization and was established as a well-accomplished yogi. Still, his meditation, scriptural study and spiritual discussions continued undeviated from their true course.

Shri Sanyal Mahasaya worked as a schoolteacher and, together with future Nobel laureate Rabindranath Tagore, founded an Institution in Shantiniketan, which later on, turned into a famous University. Shri Sanyal Mahasaya worked there from 1902 until 1909; Due to his talent, skills, exemplary character and insight he became a close associate of Tagore.

In 1910 he went to Puri, Orissa, for the first time. The holy atmosphere of this place of pilgrimage attracted him so greatly that during his life he visited Puri several times.

Shri Sanyal Mahasaya was blessed with two sons and four daughters. The two sons excelled in their education and in spiritual life. In due course they also became *acharyas* in the Kriya Yoga tradition.

In 1923, Shri Sanyal Mahasaya established Gurudham, an ashram in Puri, and in 1924 he established another ashram in Bhagalpur, in the state of Bihar. These two ashrams became the main centers of his activity. He initiated thousands of seekers into the path of Kriya Yoga, and served as their divine guide.

Shri Sanyal Mahasaya was a gifted writer. He wrote commentaries in Bengali on the Bhagavad Gita and a good number of other spiritual books, which are outstandingly unique. These books have been also translated into many other Indian languages.

On the 7th of November 1959, his wife passed away. On the 18th of January 1962, Shri Sanyal Mahasaya entered into *mahasamadhi*. His entire life was a period of great activity. Although he was a householder and was a good father to his six children, he devoted his whole life to spiritual practice and to the spreading of Kriya Yoga. He was a very simple and beautiful person, like a great *rishi* from ancient times living in the modern world. Many people are not aware of him because he was a silent worker, but there is no doubt he was a great yogi, a divine guide and guru, the author of many spiritual books, a householder, an educator, and a true lover of mankind. He was instrumental in guiding countless householders, *brahmacharis*, and monks into spiritual life.

Among his disciples, Jwala Prasad Tiwari, Nikhil Brahmachari, his two sons Kashipati and Girijapati, and our beloved Gurudeva Paramahamsa Hariharananda, have become instruments in genuinely spreading the sacred science of Kriya Yoga to sincere seekers.

DIVINE TEACHINGS OF SHRI SANYAL MAHASAYA

One must not practice yoga only by reading books, it does not provide the benefit one can get from the direct guidance of a teacher.

For the practice of yoga and meditation, there are three important requirements:
a sense of morality;
mind control;
knowledge or intelligence.

A sincere teacher can show others the right path to spiritual enlightenment.

A sincere and worthy teacher is the real guide, whereas a materialistic, greedy person is like a blind man unable to show others the right way.

One who is blessed with the eye of wisdom is free from all doubts, confusion and duality.

Strong desire, keeping good company and practice are the three steps for quick spiritual evolution.

To comprehend the subtle spiritual truth, citta (memory) must be free from impurities and imbalances through the practice of meditation. Only in this way can one enter into the state of realization.

Pranayama (simple Kriya breathing) can remove all inner impurities.

Keep control over your tongue, to gain control over your life.

Analysis (vichara), detachment (vairagya) and good company (satsanga) are helpful to attain steady spiritual growth.

To possess more and more wealth and to accumulate more and more material objects is the natural tendency of man. To earn money is difficult, to protect and preserve one's possessions is troublesome, and to loose them or have them damaged brings also a feeling of misery.

Purity in thought, refraining from criticizing others, and freedom from vanity and ego are essential in spiritual life.

Contentment is the best policy in life.

To be unaffected by the dualities of life, like pleasure and pain, loss and gain, praise and condemnation, heat and cold is the real proof of spiritual advancement.

Study the scriptures, which increase your depth and understanding and encourage you to be steady in your practice.

When a thought comes to your mind, think of God.

When your body is steady and straight, your breath will become rhythmical and your life will be beautiful.

Breath and mind are correlated. When your mind is restless, your breath is restless. A restless mind causes pain.

Have compassion for all living beings.

Never create a sense of fear in others, refrain from using harsh words.

To be truthful in words is to reveal what one has seen or heard, without adding your own perceptions.

Truth means not to allow any falsehood in thought, words or deeds.

Truth is not to hurt others.

Practice observing silence or speak only a little.

Where there are many words, mistakes are inevitable.

True penance is to endure the dualities in life like heat and cold, pleasure and pain, loss and gain, praise and censure.

Push yourself to sit in one position longer and practice meditation.

A restless mind is impure.

The purpose of breath-control is to keep the body and mind free from negative vibrations.

As fire purifies metal, breath-control purifies the mind and the senses.

Because of restless breath, mind cannot remain steady at any fixed point.

Vital breath (energy of prana) is the supreme power of man.

The gayatri mantra in the form of inhalation and exhalation can give you liberation.

When one practices breath-control through Kriya, one enjoys a blissful state and one becomes free from ego.

Remember, one day or another you will leave this world, do not run madly after material things.

Through sadhana (spiritual discipline) one will get peace.

Seek a secluded place for your spiritual practice.

Man has enough time for self-development. Start now!

Forbearance is the best policy in life.

Keep your mind concentrated and your senses under control.

Regular and sincere practice brings success.

Keep your mind always in tune with the scriptures and the teachings of the Master.

Without patience one cannot progress on the spiritual path.

Through spiritual evolution one becomes free from the torture of passion, anger and greed.

Direct your mind to think of nothing but your soul, and then concentrate on each exhalation and inhalation.

Eat only upto half of your stomach's capacity, leaving the rest for water and air. Practice moderation.

In order to achieve samadhi (realization), have strong self-control in every aspect, practice steadiness of mind, put your faith in the scriptures and your guru, accompany this with devotion, compassion for others, and remain non-attached.

Paramahamsa Yogananda

A LIFE OF LOVE AND LIBERATION

Love is often a topic for discussions, but is love merely a word? Can love be possessive or selfish? Is love no more than sacrifice? Love is inner fulfillment. Love is a manifestation of purity, divinity and liberty in every step of life, in every moment of time. Love is the experience of our divine nature. Love is the supreme purifier. Love transforms life. Love never fails.

"One who jumps into the ocean of love dies and survives at the same time", sang a poet-saint in divine ecstasy. When immersed in real love one's ego dies, but one lives in purity and perfection. That love can conquer everything is not a mere way of saying, but it is widely exemplified through the lives of great saints, exceptional souls as Paramahamsa Yogananda, a great gift of God to Humanity. His life and teachings, through his writings and his divine messages, still thrill the hearts of people with love and devotion.

Born on the 5th of January 1893, during a chilly winter, at the foothill of the Himalayas in the holy city of Gorakhpur, he came to warm not only the lives of his own parents, but also of mankind. Mukunda, later known as Paramahamsa Yogananda, became a spiritual dynamo known throughout the world. Bhagavati Charan Ghosh and Gyana Prabha Ghosh, his devoted parents, whose lives had already been transformed through the divine touch of Shri Lahiri Mahasaya, were instrumental in providing an environment for the evolution of the body, mind and spirit of this child.

Bhagavati Charan Ghosh led an honest, strict and disciplined life. Gyana Prabha was an extremely pious lady with a kind and tender heart, which kindled the spark of love in the life of the child Mukunda. This type of environment and opportunity fulfills the declaration of the Lord in the Bhagavad Gita VI/42, that a yogi, a spiritually advanced soul, is born into a family of yogis, getting ample opportunity for self-evolution and advancement.

THE PROPHECY

Shri Lahiri Mahasaya whose life was a symbol of the integration of action and renunciation, was the guru and guide of Bhagavati and Gyana Prabha. It is a customary tradition in India to offer one's baby at the feet of the guru for blessings and purification. The divine parents took Mukunda to their beloved guru when he was just a baby, Lahiri held him lovingly in his arms and blessed him with spoken and unspoken words. Shri Lahiri Mahasaya was a divine touchstone with transforming powers. It is an old legendary belief that a touchstone can transform ordinary metal into gold, so when the divine guru is that touchstone, through the power of his divine love and grace, disciples are transformed.

This great yogi, with deep insight and intuition could easily see the past, present and future. He looked at Mukunda's eyes and forehead and forecast; "This is not an ordinary child. He is blessed with supremely divine qualities. He is here with a great mission to fulfill. One day, this child will become a spiritual engine to carry many seeking souls to the feet of the Lord, with love and care". The prophecy of this great divine guru proved to be true and his blessings were always with Mukunda throughout his life.

"MY GOLDFISH DIED"

As morning shows the day, the child Mukunda was quite unusual in his behaviour, talk and outlook. In his family yard there was a water reservoir for emergency use. Mukunda had a tiny goldfish that he kept in that reservoir. For many hours a day he would sit watching the goldfish because it made him enjoy the divine bliss of the ocean of the cosmic consciousness and love. One day the family servant used some water from the reservoir to clean the house and the goldfish, which had accidentally been picked up, died when the water was thrown on the floor. When Mukunda returned from school, he went to the reservoir to see his fish, but as it was no longer there, he searched and searched everywhere. When he discovered it was dead, tears rolled down his cheeks and he could not even eat his dinner. That night he drew a picture of the goldfish and wrote, "My goldfish died" and he fell asleep with his head on the picture. Divinely intoxicated people have love for all living creatures. Mukunda's heart was overflowing with love.

A LETTER TO GOD

When people write letters to their friends and relatives, they expect a reply, so when they arrive home from work they usually check if they have any mail. Mukunda loved God as his father, mother, friend and relative. He believed that God was very close, so he thought of writing a letter to Him. He spent some nights writing this letter, expressing how he loved God and how he expected to obtain God's vision and *darshan*. He sealed his letter and addressed the envelope to: "God, in Heaven", without forgetting to write his return address, and with postage paid, and then he mailed the letter. Every day upon his return from school, he would go and see if a reply had arrived.

When the postman saw the letter, he was very surprised and took it to the postmaster who knew Mukunda's father. The postmaster returned the letter in a different envelope to Bhagavati Charan Ghosh, who was not at all surprised as he well knew the heart of his son, and had always encouraged his sincere search and love for God.

THE SPARK OF LOVE

Mukunda's mother was extremely loving and dear to him. Although she died when he was only eleven years old, she set alight the spark of love for the Divine Mother in her son. This love increased day by day, as did his prayer, meditation and passion for divine experience.

During his youth Mukunda was always searching for opportunities to visit holy men and their kind words, loving and caring touch made a great difference in his life. During this time Mukunda also encouraged and inspired some of his friends to lead a really spiritual life following strict disciplines.

A LEADER FROM CHILDHOOD

Mukunda always took the lead in various events. He was the leader of a soccer team and thanks to this common past time, he met his spiritual companion Manmohan, who would later be known as Swami Satyananda. Mukunda and Manmohan lived in the same neighbourhood, so they spent many nights meditating together. Another friend, Basukumar Bagchi, later became Swami Dhirananda.

Although born into a very rich family, where he could have ample opportunities for 'so-called' enjoyment, Mukunda's mind always strove for self-mastery. He was extremely kind-hearted and always wanted to distribute and share all what he had, be it material belongings or spiritual wisdom. Even as a schoolboy, when he learned the art of meditation through his initial Kriya practice, he did not keep it secret, but shared it with his friends.

HIS EARLY GURUS

In his childhood, he learned some techniques of Kriya from his father, who was his first guru of Kriya and developed his interest in meditation. As a high school boy, Mukunda was not so devoted to his studies, so he usually had to resort to private tutors. Among them was the great Sanskrit scholar Ashutosh Mukhopadhyaya, also known as Shastri Mahasaya and later on as Hamsa Swami Kevalananda. He was chosen by Mukunda's elder brother, Ananta, to teach him Sanskrit, even if Ananta did not know that this saintly man was really an elevated spiritual Master, a disciple of Shri Lahiri Mahasaya. Locked up in a room, while the family thought that they might be discussing school subjects or Sanskrit, Mukunda was learning about spiritual truth, meditation and the intricacies that lie behind the different scriptures. Thus, Mukunda got the revered spiritual teacher he had desired and prayed for, who taught him not only Sanskrit but also Kriya meditation and the Bhagavad Gita.

MEETING WITH SHRIYUKTESHWAR

Swami Shriyukteshwar was at this time a full fledged spiritual Master, well-established in the Karar ashram in Puri, Orissa. He used to spend four months in Puri, four months in Serampore, his birthplace and four months in Benares, the place of his guru Shri Lahiri Mahasaya. In a divinely ordained situation, Mukunda came into contact with Swami Shriyukteshwar in Benares in 1910 and this meeting ended his search for a spiritual Master who could guide and shape his life. The foundation for his Kriya practice, which had been laid by the teachings of his own father-guru and Kevalananda, became reinforced by Shriyukteshwar's strict disciplined instructions. Mukunda managed to spend most of his time in the company of his divine guru and from 1910 to 1915, under the pretext of receiving higher education, he lived most of the time in Serampore. Although he did not care for a University degree since his heart was set in becoming a monk, Shriyukteshwar motivated him to complete his education, with Philosophy as His major subject. In June 1915, Mukunda obtained his final degree from the University and in the following month he was ordained by his beloved guru into the monastic life of the Giri order. Henceforth Mukunda Ghosh became known as Swami Yogananda Giri.

A LIFE OF MEDITATION AND RIGHT ACTION

Yogananda and his friends started their own spiritual group in Calcutta, with a dream of eventually opening a *brahmacharya vidyalaya*, a school for strictly celibate students. They founded an ashram in Dihika, in the state of Bengal, and later on moved to Ranchi, in the state of Bihar. Yogananda's dream-like-vision and Satyananda's hard work made it possible to build and maintain this ashram and school. They were blessed with a generous donation from Yogananda's father and even from the King Mahendra Chandra Nandi of Kasimbazar, Bengal. Their main activity was caring for the sick and poor and helping children, from extremely poor localities, obtain their only chance for education, enriched with meditation and spiritual values.

When the great spiritual leader of India, Mahatma Gandhi, visited the beautiful ashram and school, he bestowed on it his admiration and highest esteem.

MESSENGER TO THE WEST

Swami Yogananda always dreamed of going to the West. First of all, he received a scholarship and a job offer in Japan. Without the consent of Shriyukteshwar, he went to Japan, but did not stay long, as he soon felt the urge to return to India. Shortly afterwards, he lost his eldest brother, Ananta, who had been instrumental as a medium for testing Yogananda's trust in God in various situations. In 1920, Yogananda was invited to attend the Congress of Religions, in Boston and this was the occasion in which he received the direct blessings of Shri Babaji to go to America.

In America, he travelled far and wide, delivering lectures and creating a receptive environment for spiritual life. At that time, people in the West were not familiar with meditation and the yogic lifestyle. Yogananda was one of the first pioneers from India who helped to open westerners mind to a new concept of spirituality. He was the first to introduce Kriya Yoga and to explain the yogic way of life in such an accessible and beautiful way that he reached many of his American disciples' hearts. His strong will power, dynamic personality, divine love and high state of spiritual experience, enabled him to be a spiritual dynamo that encouraged and inspired millions of people. His work was progressing at such a galloping pace that it was difficult for him to work alone, so he tried to invite Swami Satyananda to come and join him in his divine mission, but Swami Satyananda declined, saying that his place was in India.

Later on Swami Dhirananda, formerly Basukumar Bagchi, left India to go to assist Yogananda who, once more, had to resort to Satyananda's help asking Him to train new brahmacharis and disciples so that they could be ready to help him in his work in the United States. In 1928, Brahmachari Jatin, who was later ordained as Swami Premananda, went to America. Eventually Yogananda found the Church of Self

Realization in Washington D.C. and became the author of many interesting spiritual books.

Yogananda's beloved guru, Swami Shriyukteshwar, was always proud of the success his dearest disciple was having in the West, but he would often request Yogananda to return to India. In 1935, after a decade and a half of tireless work, Yogananda made the trip back to India, stopping in Europe on the way.

The joy of the reunion between Yogananda and Shriyukteshwar and Yogananda and his father, Bhagavati Charan, cannot be expressed in words. While he was in India for several months, he also had the opportunity to visit many spiritual leaders, met Mahatma Gandhi and initiated him and many of his followers into the sacred technique of Kriya Yoga. He visited Ramana Maharshi, Anandamoyee Ma and many disciples of Shri Lahiri Mahasaya including his saintly wife, Kashimani Devi.

In the many places he visited all over India, Yogananda was received with great honour and respect. It was during this period, that he also initiated Paramahamsa Hariharananda, our Gurudev, into second Kriya in Calcutta. In January 1936, Yogananda visited the *Kumbha Mela*, the holy gathering of monks, spiritual teachers and saints, in Allahabad, where the three sacred rivers, Ganga, Yamuna and invisible Saraswati merge.

FROM SWAMI TO PARAMAHAMSA

During his visit to India Swami Sriyukteshwar honoured Yogananda by conferring on him the highest monastic title of Paramahamsa. A Paramahamsa, the "supreme swan", is one whose mind is always engrossed in the Lord and His divine play, being inwardly detached from all occurrences. From that time onwards, Yogananda came to be known as Paramahamsa Yogananda.

MAHASAMADHI OF SHRIYUKTESHWAR

When Yogananda was at the *Kumbha Mela* and later on in Calcutta, for the festival of Holi, the festival of colour celebrating Lord Krishna, he received several calls from Shriyukteshwar asking him to return to Puri, but as Yogananda was planning to combine his visit to Puri with the foundation-day celebration of the Karar ashram, on the day of the vernal equinox, the 22nd of March, he delayed his visit. On the 9th of March 1936, Shriyukteshwar sent an urgent message to Paramahamsa Yogananda to come back to Puri immediately and on the same day, in the evening, he consciously left his physical body.

The next morning Yogananda reached Puri with the intuitive knowledge of Shriyukteshwar's *mahasamadhi*. It is difficult to describe the sorrow of the realized yogi, who had lost the physical company and guidance of his beloved guru. According to tradition, a monk's body is not burned, it is buried. Yogananda performed the burial ceremony on the ashram premises and, as per the tradition, organised a *bhandara*, inviting several monks of Puri and many well-known spiritual leaders to pay tribute to this great guru.

After a couple of months he decided to leave India to fulfill his divine mission in the West, but before leaving India on the 19th of June, while he was staying in a room at the Regent Hotel in Bombay, Yogananda had the rare opportunity of experiencing the actual materialization of Shriyukteshwar, who appeared to him in bodily form. This was a mesmerising and inspiring encounter with his loving guru.

DIVINE PREDICTION

Swami Vivekananda, who was the chief monastic disciple of Shri Ramakrishna Paramahamsa, a great spiritual Master of the last century, was the first messenger to extend India's spiritual treasure and tradition to the West. He was a delegate to the Parliament of Religions, held in Chicago, in September 1893, which was incidentally also the year when Paramahamsa Yogananda was born.

Dickinson, a young man of seventeen, was miraculously drawn to this august gathering without any prior knowledge of it. Looking at the smiling and loving Swami Vivekananda, he intuitively knew that here was someone that would save his life on many occasions. He approached Swamiji wishing to become his disciple, but Swami Vivekananda lovingly patted the young man and said, "My child! I am not your guru. Your guru will come from India later on". The young man asked, "How will I recognize him?" to which Vivekananda replied, "He will fill your life and heart with love and divinity and he will give you, as a present, a silver cup". Dickinson did not disclose these words to anybody but treasured them in his heart. As the years passed, he waited and prayed every day to meet his spiritual teacher as prophesied by the great saint. In 1925, his prayers were answered. He met Paramahamsa Yogananda who was at that time teaching in Los Angeles. Dickinson started to practice Kriya Yoga under Yogananda's guidance and grew in love and inner spiritual experience. But where was the silver cup? He consoled himself with the thought that it might have been only a metaphor.

On Christmas day in 1936, after returning from his trip to India, Paramahamsa Yogananda was joyfully offering presents to his disciples. He presented Dickinson with a gift he had purchased at a Calcutta market, with a remark that he might like it. The parcel contained a silver cup. Tears of joy and gratitude streamed from the eyes of the man, who was now nearly 60 years old. Dickinson had been waiting for 43 years to see Vivekananda's words come true.

In the year of birth of Paramahamsa Yogananda, Swami Vivekananda had already foreseen the coming to the West of a great Indian yogi; thus the great divine play of God is disclosed through the life of saints and sages.

EVENTFUL LIFE

The life of Paramahamsa Yogananda was eventful and miraculous in nature. He was not only a gifted orator and singer who thrilled the hearts of his listeners, he was also an extraordinary author. Among the books that were published during his lifetime, which won the appreciation of thousands are: *Autobiography of a Yogi, Whispers From Eternity, The Science of Religion, The Divine Romance* and *Metaphysical Meditations.*

Yogananda worked ceaselessly, day and night. At midnight and even later, he was still surrounded by several secretaries taking dictation, writing and answering seekers' letters from all over the world. In one of his letters to his disciple Rabinarayan (later known as Paramahamsa Hariharananda, our beloved Gurudev), he wrote on the 6th October 1951; "My life is a whirlwind of activity and struggle with work".

HIS LAST SMILE

For a short period, at the beginning of 1952, Yogananda was very sick. On 7th of March he recovered miraculously. On that day a banquet was to take place in honour of the Ambassador of India to the United States, his Excellency Mr. Binay Ranjam Sen. During this celebration, Yogananda was full of humour and joy. No one suspected that it was his last day on earth. Many photos were taken during the reception showing him smiling and blissful. Then he sang a song glorifying India:

"*Where Ganges, woods, Himalayan caves and men dream of God;*
I am hallowed; my body touched that sod".

They were his last words, paying tribute to his motherland, which had given him his training and inspiration. Although a monk is for all humanity, Yogananda's love for India, his guru and his parents remained always unique.

He had often told his disciples: "I do not wish to die in bed but with my boots on, speaking of God and India". When he was so literal in the fulfillment of his words, his closest disciples were in a state of shock. Nobody wanted to believe or accept his death and, for several weeks, they waited for him to return to his body. There was no sign of decomposition. His face was filled with peace and calmness, like that of a sleeping child. His physical play had come to an end, and although his physical body was eventually buried, his divine play continues forever. A guru's teachings are eternal. To pay homage to the divine guru is to follow closely his teachings, imprinting in one's mind the steps that led him on the ascending path. In a letter to Brahmachari Rabinarayan, Yogananda he had written: "Do not seek to find faults in others, for then your whole life becomes tied with negative traits. Every person has some faults and needs love and understanding. Be humble and loving towards others. Keep your mind engrossed with the divine and you won't have time to think about these lesser things".

May his life of love and liberation be an example for all of us to keep our lives in tune with the Divine and by following his teachings begin our transformation in order to reach self-realization.

DIVINE TEACHINGS
OF PARAMAHAMSA YOGANANDA

God is love. His plan for creation is rooted in love.

Do not be attached to the passing dreams of life. Live only for God and God alone.

Behind the light in every little bulb is a great dynamic current; behind the waves, vast oceans, and behind the individual lies the Supreme Spirit.

The Moon is not reflected clearly in ruffled water, but only on its calm surface. True love for God is manifested through calmness of the mind.

All successful men and women spend much of their time in deep concentration.

A calm person reflects serenity in his eyes, a keen intelligence in his facial expression and an open receptiveness in his mind.

Mahavatar Babaji Maharaj

Lahiri Mahasaya

Paramahamsa Yogananda

Swami Satyananda

Paramahamsa Hariharananda

Paramahamsa Prajnanananda

Self-analysis is a secret element on the road to progress.

By drawing and observing the graph of your mind, you can see whether everyday you are making any progress in your life or not.

The wisest person seeks God; the most successful one has found Him.

Peace is the altar of God.

Calmness is the living breath of God's immortality within you.

Be introspect. Take stock of yourself and your habits and find out what is standing in your way.

Avoid a negative approach towards life.

Lack of concentration is the cause of many failures in life.

Nothing is impossible unless you think it is.

As a mortal being you are limited, but as a child of God you are unlimited.

Problems are a necessary ingredient in life and make it worthwhile. Meet everybody and every circumstance in the battlefield of life with the courage of a hero and the smile of a conqueror.

Trouble and disease have hidden lessons for us. Try to use life's experience as a guiding teacher.

Misery is really your best friend because it awakens your search for God.

Suffering is a good teacher to those who are quick and willing to learn from it.

Death means nothing to the spiritually strong.

Danger and ego were born together, but the ego is the more dangerous of the two.

Yoga is the art of doing everything in God-consciousness.

The first rule in prayer is to approach God only with legitimate desires. Pray for their fulfillment, not as a beggar but as His child.

Think and plan well before you take action, do not jump into anything at once.

Picture marriage as a laboratory experiment in which the poison of selfishness, bad temper and bad behaviour is poured into a test-tube of patience and neutralized and transformed by the catalytic power of love and constant effort in order to obtain the most noble union.

People who want to marry must learn first to control their emotions.

God is eternal bliss, infinite love, wisdom and joy.

The more peace you feel in meditation, the closer you are to God.

A successful life must begin with the cultivation of your soul.

Cleanliness is next to Godliness.

A student who changes frequently from one school to another cannot get a really good education. This also applies to the spiritual path, do not change your practice frequently or you will loose your way.

When love for all things is seen as an expression of God, man's consciousness will at last be expanded in omnipresence.

Any disturbance like disease, decay and even death are natural friends to the body.

Man stands in the middle, with God on one side and Satan on the other, each one ready to pull him in whichever direction he wishes to go.

Everyone is a potential Krishna or Christ.

To seek one's own salvation without benefiting others is extreme selfishness.

You can give only what you have.

God is the supreme cure of all illness.

A guru-preceptor will keep coming back to earth voluntarily until all his disciples have found liberation.

As a tree is known by its fruit, a teacher will be known by his students.

A flower needs no advertisement.

The body is the frozen thought and energy of God.

While promising happiness; sin really results in unhappiness.

Sickness is the result of mental or physical laws that have been broken.

Achievement lies in continuous effort and activity.

Habit governs human nature.

A seeker must fight with his senses to obtain spiritual victory.

The true secret of spiritual truth lies in the cave of stillness.

When you talk, do not speak too much of yourself, instead try to be a good listener.

Swami Satyananda

THE TRAVELLER ON THE PATH OF TRUTH

Simplicity, serenity and spirituality are reflected in the life of a great yogi. Swami Satyananda Giri was a philosopher, a singer, a composer, a poet, a social worker and above all a gifted disciple and, later on, a truly divine Master in the Lineage of Kriya Yoga. *Satya* means truth, and *ananda* means bliss. Satyananda's life, although full of trials and tribulations, never deviated from truth. His whole life was a shelter for truth. Truth was his breath. Truth was his activity. Truth always triumphs because it is eternal. Life without truth is not a divine life at all. From childhood, Swami Satyananda was a sincere seeker of truth.

His childhood name was Manmohan Mazumdar and he was the eldest son of Mohini Mohan Mazumdar and Taravasini Devi. He was born on the 17th of November 1896, at his maternal uncle's house in Bikrampur, Bangladesh. He had five brothers and one sister. His nickname during his childhood was "Khandu".

Mohini Mohan, who later on became a luminary in both the spiritual and social fields, was a person of high moral standards and a broad minded independent personality. Although artistic in nature being both a painter and a singer, he became the founder of a Deaf and Dumb School in Calcutta. He lived with his family in a house, near the institution setting for his young son a firm example of service to those in need.

A BOY WHO SHOWS GREAT PROMISE

When he was a boy of six or seven, Manmohan Mazumdar proved to be a true lover of mankind. He never accepted discrimination among people on account of caste, social status or religion. In a family gathering, where many relatives and friends had been invited, he broke the tradition of untouchability. He, with his childhood simplicity, boldly and clearly stressed that every human being was the child of God and that untouchability was a crime against God.

When he was about ten years old, Manmohan was truly fascinated by the patriotic discourses of the great national heroes and freedom fighters. Even though their fiery discourses were in English, every word created a throb in the heart of this young boy. He was not only thinking of a free and independent India, but also of freedom from bondage and suffering, in order to obtain true independence from the shackles of body consciousness.

MEETING HIS CHILDHOOD GUIDE AND FRIEND

One summer afternoon in 1906, Manmohan was standing outside the entrance of the Deaf and Dumb School, when his friend Kalinath came to borrow his hand-pump to inflate a football and thus Manmohan had the opportunity to meet Mukunda, the teenage youth who led the football team. It was at this point that Manmohan was invited to join the team and from then onwards these two young men met every afternoon and became very close friends. Mukunda was only two years older than Manmohan.

Apart from playing football, they got involved in very serious discussions about spiritual life, morality, and keeping up their high ideals in life. Mukunda expressed clearly his desire to dedicate his entire life to spiritual practice and self-realization, he believed firmly that life was not meant for eating, drinking, enjoyment, earning money and getting married to have children; it had to have a higher purpose and to this he would dedicate himself.

Mukunda was a true leader. He not only practiced Kriya Yoga and enjoyed a state of peace and bliss, he also taught his close friends the practice of meditation. Manmohan was really fortunate to have such a childhood guide to lead his first steps in spiritual life. Both friends practiced meditation in seclusion, in many holy places and temples and even at night when everyone was asleep.

The two boy's homes were just a few blocks apart. Every night, without the knowledge of their parents, they spent most of the time in deep meditation. In order to avoid sleep and drowsiness, they sometimes took a cup of hot tea. Where there is a will, there is a way. While other children spent their time playing and having fun; these two young friends spent most of their time immersed in spiritual practice and meditation. Their parents became rather concerned about their education and future, but they could never stop the children's spiritual practice. Together, Manmohan and Mukunda visited many holy men, saints and holy places. Among some of the spiritual Masters that had a strong impact on their lives were Master Mahasaya, Mahendranath Gupta, a scholar, educator, householder, disciple of Shri Ramakrishna Paramahamsa and author of the famous *Gospel of Sri Ramakrishna* and the "perfume saint", Swami Vishuddhananda Paramahamsa.

Two other friends, Basukumar Bagchi and Sisir Kumar, joined Mukunda and Manmohan in their spiritual practices. They all took a strict vow of celibacy and devoted time to physical exercise, study of the scriptures, meditation and chanting devotional songs.

While Mukunda lived in a state of total God intoxication and often neglected his formal education, Manmohan was a well-balanced young man; he never neglected his studies nor his spiritual life. He was never a disappointment to his family nor to his friends.

IN THE COMPANY OF KEVALANANDA

Hamsa Swami Kevalananda, the great Sanskrit scholar who had been Mukunda's tutor also taught Manmohan some basics of Kriya Yoga. When Mukunda asked him questions about the scriptures, spirituality and meditation, he would share these profound and amazing replies from this divine teacher, with Manmohan and then together both the students would sincerely practice Kriya and they would also serve their teacher with all their heart and soul.

The simple lifestyle and sincerity of Kevalananda had a strong influence on Manmohan's life.

Manmohan faithfully served this great yogi even in his old age and later on in life, he wrote a short biography in Bengali of his teacher who was also known as Shastri Mahasaya.

MEETING WITH SHRIYUKTESHWAR

In the meantime, Mukunda had met his destined guru, Swami Shriyukteshwar, in Benares and had accepted him as his divine guide to shape his life and help him reach the divine goal.

In the year 1911, in Calcutta, Manmohan also had the opportunity to meet Swami Shriyukteshwar and that day became the most memorable day in Manmohan's life. He was quite enthralled with the divine presence of this great guru. Shriyukteshwar's tall body, broad forehead, long and powerful arms and strong divine personality impressed him greatly.

Manmohan surrendered himself at the Master's feet and accepted him as his guru and guide. The surrender of the disciple and his acceptance by the loving Master makes the spiritual journey much easier. It is said that those who are extremely determined to reach their goal in life and who are endowed with an understanding heart are already half way and that with an able guide at their side to point the way, three-fourths of the journey is covered and that their own effort only accounts for the last quarter.

Shriyukteshwar occupied a special place in Manmohan's life and his guru's deep insight, profound metaphorical interpretation of the scriptures, divine experience in Kriya Yoga practice and knowledge of astronomy and astrology inspired this young man to be an ardent and dedicated student. That year, Manmohan graduated from high school and entered college.

IN THE ASHRAM OF BALANANDA BRAHMACHARI

In September-October, when all educational Institutions in India close for a month, the four spiritual friends decided to spend their holidays in Deoghar, in the state of Bihar. This was not only an important place of pilgrimage and a holy place with many ashrams and monasteries, but also a health resort. Deoghar was famous for being the home of two great disciples of Shri Lahiri Mahasaya: Pandit Panchanan Bhattacharya, a great householder yogi and Balananda Brahmachari, a highly accomplished and powerful yogi.

The four friends dedicated their time to meditation, keeping good company, discussing the Holy Scriptures, going for morning walks and cooking their food while Mukunda always was the source of inspiration and encouragement for all.

They sat at the feet of Balananda Brahmachari and listened to his scriptural interpretations. The disciples of Balananda Brahmachari also encouraged these young yogis to meditate deeply and to strive to reach the state of realization.

In 1915, in the month of July, when his friend Mukunda was initiated into the monastic life and became known as Swami Yogananda Giri, Manmohan was still a student at the University, majoring in Philosophy.

STARTING THEIR OWN ASHRAM

On the 22nd of March 1917, Basukumar, Swami Yogananda and Manmohan, under the patronage of King Mahendra Chandra Nandi, started an ashram and a residential school with a strict spiritual discipline, first in Dihika, and then in Ranchi. During that same year, Basukumar Bagchi accepted the life of renunciation and was reborn under the name of Swami Dhirananda.

The following year, Manmohan graduated from the University with a B.A. honours degree. Manmohan was a hard worker endowed with devotion, dedication, determination and discipline. Finally, in March

1919, under the direction of Swami Shriyukteshwar, Manmohan was initiated into the monastic order. He became known as Swami Satyananda Giri. His childhood dream, which started with the inspiration of his friend Yogananda, became a reality the day he became a swami.

A monk's life is not an outward show or governed by exhibitionism, it is a life of sacrifice and surrender to the divine will. As monks, Swami Satyananda and Swami Dhirananda spent all their time and energy meditating and organizing the residential ashram school in Ranchi. Through their hard work the school achieved great popularity and success. Although Swami Satyananda was of a serious disposition, he treated his students with so much love and care that even ordinary students were moved to do their very best.

WITH MAHATMA GANDHI

Mahatma Gandhi, the great inspiring force for India's independence, a humanist, the most convincing advocate of peace and non-violence (*ahimsa*) in the modern world, a true leader of the nation, was a spiritual giant. While touring India to raise his countrymen's self-reliance and self-esteem, in order to secure independence through peace, the Mahatma also went to Ranchi. He had heard about the sincere work of a few young monks, who were preaching and teaching the illiterate children of the local tribal population. Fascinated, he visited the ashram in Ranchi and participated in the daily activities of the ashram and school. He was extremely pleased with the service rendered there. He also came to know about the work of Yogananda in America.

The exemplary character, simplicity and honesty of Satyananda, his love and care for each student, were the special feature and a source of inspiration for both students and teachers of this school. Realizing the constructive work of Swami Satyananda, Gandhi invited him to come to his own Sabaramati ashram. Satyananda visited Gandhi's ashram in 1927. He was warmly welcomed by Gandhi and was requested to stay in the ashram for a long period of time and as

Satyananda did not like to be treated as a guest of an ashram, he followed all the activities and principles of the ashram like any normal and regular initiate. At that time, Gandhi and some of his followers discussed Kriya Yoga in detail with Swami Satyananda. Later on in 1935, when Yogananda returned to India and had the opportunity to visit Gandhi's ashram, Gandhi took Kriya Yoga initiation from him.

ASHRAM SWAMI

During 1935 and 1936, the two childhood friends met again, after a long physical separation that had lasted fifteen years. No words can describe this reunion. True friendship, based on love and sacrifice, is eternal. Yogananda reiterated the open invitation for Satyananda to come to the United States and help him in his divine mission in the West, but Satyananda sadly declined.

Meanwhile, the Karar ashram in Puri had become a model for spiritual seekers who wished to devote themselves to the practice of Kriya Yoga. Following the call of Shriyukteshwar, Swami Satyananda went to Puri and lived there under the spiritual guidance of his divine guru. Shriyukteshwar installed Swami Satyananda as the ashram swami.

On the 9th of March 1936, the beloved Master, Swami Shriyukteshwar entered into *mahasamadhi*. After a few months Yogananda left India again for America. A few years later Swami Satyananda initiated Brahmachari Rabinarayan (our beloved Gurudev) into higher Kriya at the Karar ashram. In 1940, being relieved from work and management of the ashram, Swami Satyananda accepted the life of a wandering monk, preaching and teaching the practical aspect of Kriya Yoga all over India and inspiring thousands to follow the spiritual path.

A LIFE OF SERVICE AND LOVE

During his *parivrajaka*, wandering monk's life in South India, he came to the ashram of Ramana Maharshi, a great luminary, renowned for his deep spiritual experience and very unusual way of teaching the process of self-enquiry through inner silence. The meeting of Ramana Maharshi and Swami Satyananda was an indescribably unique one. When they met, they immediately and deeply loved each other. Maharshi pressed Swami Satyananda to settle down in his ashram permanently, but the divine plan was different.

In 1944, during a terrible famine in Bengal, Swami Satyananda's desire to serve the poor brought him back to the north east corner of India in answer to the call of a starving and dying population. His motto was: "Service with love and meditation for all". The ideal of this great saint was to work until his last breath for the physical, moral and spiritual upliftment of mankind.

He returned to Bengal and selected the most undeveloped area, Jhargram, in the Midnapur district, as his last place of work. This was the foundation of the Sevayatan Satsang Mission, where he spent most of the latter part of his life from 1944 until 1971, transforming the life of thousands of people. In 1952, the news of the *mahasamadhi* of his childhood friend and guide, Yogananda, was a great shock for him. From that time on, until the end of his life, he also became the president of the Karar ashram in Puri.

Swami Satyananda was simultaneously a writer, a composer, a singer, a poet, a servant of the downtrodden, an educator, a moralist and a spiritual Master. He wrote the original biographies of Shri Lahiri Mahasaya, Shriyukteshwar, Hamsa Swami Kevalananda and also the memories of his association with Paramahamsa Yogananda (*Yogananda Sanga*). He was a poet of extraordinary caliber and he wrote many poems based on Kriya practice and the yogic life style. His voice was extremely melodious and divine.

He led a full life. He was the head of two Institutions until his death; the Karar ashram in Puri and the Sevayatan Satsang Mission in Jhargram.

Although he suffered from heart trouble since 1934, he managed to work hard and devotedly until 1971. On the 2nd of August of that year, he left his mortal body in Sevayatan, Jhargram, Bengal.

Thousands of disciples and devotees gathered to pay homage to this great soul.

In Puri, his dear disciple Brahmachari Rabinarayan (our beloved Gurudev, Paramahamsa Hariharananda), and in Jhargram, his younger brother, Swami Shuddhananda inherited the responsibility of carrying on his mission. In his will, he appointed them both to succeed him in these two separate Institutions.

Life is not measured in years and months, but by the work performed with devotion. The life of a lamp burning in the night to dispel darkness is far better than a long-lasting fire covered with smoke and ashes. The life of Swami Satyananda is an ideal of love, simplicity, activity, devotion and realization for all. In his childhood he followed Paramahamsa Yogananda, in his youth Swami Kevalananda and as an adult Swami Shriyukteshwar. He dedicated his life to guiding thousands of people on the path of love and truth. He loved truth, lived in truth and realized truth in his life.

DIVINE TEACHINGS OF SWAMI SATYANANDA

My only teaching is "Love all".

Through one's character the humanity in man flourishes.

Being a sthita prajna (established in wisdom) is the true state of spiritual growth.

When one walks with faith in God one can perceive the presence of the guru's grace within.

We need a guide and teacher in spiritual life just as much as in material life.

Whatever pressing engagement a person might have, if he is able to sit silently for a while, he will get great strength.

The seed of devotion and faith is hidden in the heart of all. Good company, spiritual discussions, and self-analysis are essential for the development of the plant.

When one sincerely strives for inner fulfillment for a good period of time one progresses in the path of perfection. Then one attains self-realization.

Just as one focuses one's energy to succeed in school and later on in college, one must also try to gain physical, mental and spiritual development.

Work for work's sake, not to obtain a result.

If a kriyavan does not practice Kriya, it means he is not feeding the inner guru established already in the heart. So, if you are keeping the guru unfed, would you take food?

Never consider yourself as the doer in any action.

Every karma (action) has a twofold result; one enjoyed in this life, and the other deposited for the next life.

Even if you are well-educated, never think of yourself as a knowledgeable person.

Remember that you are to learn from one and all.

Scholarship of the scriptures is of little significance. Was Ramakrishna Paramahamsa a great scholar? Yet every word from his mouth was a scripture.

Until and unless one is established in the Self, one has no right to give spiritual advice to others.

Veda means knowledge. One who knows the Self is a true scholar of the Vedas or scriptures.

Do not consider the fault of others.

Never accuse others of their mistakes. If a person has only one good quality out of 100 then try to see that good one not the 99 bad ones.

Man is the manifestation of both good and bad qualities. In some people, good prevails whereas in others evil is predominant.

In God's creation good and bad, light and darkness, are always present.

Man, due to ignorance, commits mistakes.

The existence of the Self is the true miracle within you. If you do not realize your "Self", then you do not do yourself justice.

It is easy to renounce the family and the world, but difficult to renounce the ego that is so firmly established and so willing to grow.

Always be humble and meek.

One who forbears survives, one who cannot forbear will perish.

Practice (abhyasa) means to be established in the "atom-point".

First practice and then preach.

No work is too small; whatever you do accomplish it with faith, love and sincerity.

Every work is an opportunity to worship the divine.

Before doing any karma (action), one should discriminate if by this action one is going to get any real development.

If one does everything with the attitude of seva (service), one will enjoy real peace.

Do not crave to know more and more, rather practice to get perfection and through the instruction of the guru, eventually, everything will become clear.

In order to keep the body and the mind healthy, the first step is to keep the digestive system in good condition.

The food we consume should be suitable for physical, mental, and spiritual growth.

One must learn the technique of Kriya Yoga directly from a qualified teacher.

Through discipline one obtains self-improvement.

The practice of Kriya is the practice of self-analysis.

Through the practice of Kriya it is natural to become established in self-knowledge.

The Self or soul is the true guide.

A person is able to progress in every aspect of life when she or he practices the teachings of the Master with faith and love and incorporates them in daily life.

Make an effort to study the scriptures related to self-knowledge and to discuss the teachings of the Masters.

Your mind is the natural environment for spiritual progress.

Through practice of breath-control one becomes free from a restless mind and a restless existence.

Breath and mind are correlated. When the restlessness of prana disappears, life becomes divine.

Breath is the manifestation of the divine.

There are different levels of spiritual experience.

The realized ones might still face difficult situations; but, will remain undisturbed.

Our beloved Gurudev

Paramahamsa Hariharananda

RIVER OF COMPASSION

Paramahamsa Hariharananda, was one of the greatest realized Kriya Yoga Masters. He was a legend among spiritual seekers. He attained *nirvikalpa samadhi*, the state of no pulse and no breath, of total cessation of all activities of body, mind, thought, intellect and ego, completely merged and absorbed in God. *Nirvikalpa samadhi* is the much cherished goal of all aspirants on the spiritual path.

He was born on the 27th of May 1907, in the hamlet of Habibpur, on the bank of the sacred river Ganga, in the district of Nadia, West Bengal, just a few kilometres away from the birthplace of Shri Chaitanya Mahaprabhu. The village of Habibpur was sanctified by the birth of this holy child, whose childhood name was Rabindranath. His father Haripada Bhattacharjee was a disciplined, dedicated, devout and determined brahmin, well-versed in all Hindu scriptures. His mother Nabinkali Devi, was an outstandingly pious, generous and loving lady.

Endowed with an uncommon and marvelous brainpower, he memorized all the intricate mantras, hymns and prayers in Sanskrit while he was still a young child. At the age of eleven, he took the vow of *brahmacharya*, in the *upanayana* ceremony of the brahmins. With an ever increasing desire for spiritual progress, he went to Shri Bijay Krishna Chattopadhyaya, a householder and a realized Master living in Howrath, on the West side of Calcutta, and took initiation into the path of Jnana Yoga at the age of twelve. He went on to excel in both sacred and secular education and became well-placed in society as a technocrat.

However, his thirst for spiritual enlightenment could not be quenched by material achievement. His first guru, knowing his role was over, with divine intuition encouraged him to meet

Shriyukteshwar, the most worthy disciple of the great Master of Kriya Yoga, Lahiri Mahasaya. As advised, he called on Shriyukteshwar at his Serampore ashram in 1932, and at last received initiation into Kriya Yoga, the sacred and scientific meditation technique.

This encounter changed his life forever. Under his divine guru's practical guidance, he learnt astrology, astronomy and palmistry, along with strict discipline and meditation. He was a gifted student and made rapid progress. In 1935, when Paramahamsa Yogananda returned to India from the United States, Rabindranath was blessed to witness Yogananda's state of *samadhi* and he was initiated by him into second Kriya.

Shriyukteshwar had the wish that this young celibate renounce material life and one day take charge of his ashram in Puri. In 1938, by God's will, Rabindranath moved to the Land of *Lord Jagannath*, the seaside city of Puri, in Eastern India. At a later stage he lived permanently in Karar ashram, accepting asceticism and taking the new name of Brahmachari Rabinarayan.

It was at this point that he became wholly involved in a very strict spiritual practice of sincere meditation, observing silence for several years. Within a short time, he attained perfection in three yogic mudras: *khechari*, *bhramari* and *shambhavi*. Having achieved this spiritual stage, a supernatural divine light or aura started to emanate from his body. This phenomenon was observed by many.

In the early 1940's, Swami Satyananda Giri initiated him into third Kriya. Subsequently he learnt all the other higher Kriyas from Shrimat Bhupendranath Sanyal, popularly known as Sanyal Mahasaya. Paramahamsa Hariharananda was the divine link between all the great Masters of Kriya Yoga as he received various steps of Kriya initiations by all the living Masters.

In the mid 1940's, a young, anonymous and mysterious yogi, who unexpectedly appeared in Karar ashram, revealed the most secret technique of *samadhi* to him. During this period he attained six stages of *samadhi*. Finally in 1948, he was blessed with the highest spiritual attainment, the state of *nirvikalpa samadhi* (breathless state with no pulse) and reached the Paramahamsa stage.

During these years period of concentrated spiritual practice in order to attain a divine state of perfection, he also improved and enlarged the premises of Karar ashram and the Samadhi Temple built in honour of Shriyukteshwar.

In the late 1940's, the divine incarnation, Mahavatar Babaji, one day miraculously appeared in Rabinarayan's closed living room and again in his personal meditation room on the premises of Karar ashram. While Babaji Maharaj was blessing him, he expressed satisfaction with Rabinarayan's spiritual practice and attainment. During this crucial encounter Babaji also predicted that Rabinarayan would become his divine instrument to propagate Kriya Yoga in the East and in the West.

In the meantime, following the tradition of service to those in need, Rabinarayan kept many helpless orphan children in the ashram who, under his loving care and guidance, in the course of time became well-educated and found their rightful place in society.

In 1951, Paramahamsa Yogananda empowered him to initiate sincere seekers into Kriya Yoga. From that time onwards he started teaching the divine technique of Kriya Yoga to thousands of people, leading them along the spiritual path.

He made his life a synthesis of *karma* (action), *jnana* (knowledge) and *bhakti* (devotion) and above all he became an exemplary yogi. He often meditated through the night before his presiding deity Mother Kali, a form of the formless Divine Mother. Then, in an unusual event filled with wonder on the 27th of September, 1958, the Divine Mother appeared before him with all Her radiant splendour and graced him with blessings and directed him to spread the divine mission for the spiritual upliftment of mankind.

In the Indian tradition, a *brahmachari* ultimately becomes a swami. On the same day of his birthday, on the 27th of May, the Shankaracharya of Gobardhan Pith in Puri, Jagadguru Shrimat Swami Bharati Krishna Teerthajee Maharaj initiated him into the life of *sannyas* or complete renunciation. In 1959 Rabinarayan abandoned the white clothes of a brahmachari and from then always only wore saffron ones. Hariharananda means divine bliss that comes from the absolute formless God.

In 1960, cherishing a desire in his heart to see Babaji once more, he started towards Ranikhet, the place where Shyama Charan was initiated. As he was taking a rest on the way he heard Babaji's voice saying, "Hariharananda, why are you taking so much trouble to come here? I will appear before you in your guru's hermitage. When I feel it, I will appear before you on my own. I am ever satisfied with you. You will inundate the Western countries with the streams of Kriya Yoga. Go back. You will not get my vision here".

Hariharananda has been blessed also by many God-intoxicated divine persons, like Anandamoyee Ma and Nanga Baba Digambara Paramahamsa, a naked and realized Master living in the outskirts of Puri near Lokanath Temple.

He dedicated most of his time to the teaching and preaching of Kriya Yoga. People of all castes, creeds and social strata gathered around him to hear his divine interpretation of the scriptures in a new metaphorical way. He started touring different parts of India, extending the Kriya Yoga 'network' throughout the country.

In the early 1970's there was a Conference of World Religions at Barabati Stadium, in Cuttack, under the auspices of the Divine Life Society, a leading spiritual organization. The venue was packed with people from different parts of the world, a spiritual audience of several thousands. Hariharananda delivered two speeches in English; *The Essence of All Religions* and *The Message of Spiritual Life*. All the monks and renowned intellectuals who were present were amazed at his brilliant and convincing presentation. Thereafter many spiritual organizations made a point, to invite him to their ashrams to give lectures and to bless and grace devotees with his divine message.

From then onwards, hundreds of people from different parts of the world gathered at Shriyukteshwar's ashram in Puri and accepted Swami Hariharananda as their divine guide, their true Master. When his message spread to the West, many of the kriyavans who met him, insistently and repeatedly requested him to go to Europe and America. It became evident that there was great work ahead and it would require extraordinary energy in order to make the extrovert and restless minds of the Western people introvert and tranquil and help them advance spiritually by experiencing inner calmness through breath-control.

Eventually, in 1974, Baba Hariharananda could no longer deny his destiny, he had to carry out a divine mission. He first went to Switzerland and later on to Germany, France, Holland, Belgium, England and many other European countries. In 1975, he travelled as far as the United States and Canada and was warmly welcomed even in South America. For over twenty years he ceaselessly and selflessly travelled all around the world and at the same time inspired many of his disciples to carry on his divine mission of spreading Kriya message all over the world.

Since then thousands of people in the West were transformed by his message. Through his divine touch, a sincere disciple could experience three divine perceptions – seeing the divine light, hearing the divine sound and feeling a divine sensation in the whole body. Anyone who came into his presence with purity in his mind and in his heart was transformed by his touch.

He was well-versed in the Vedas, the Upanishads, the Bhagavad Gita, the Brahmasutra, Smrutisastras, Karmakanda and other Holy Indian Scriptures. He also had a thorough knowledge of the Torah, the Holy Bible, the Koran, the Buddhist Scriptures and ethical and metaphysical teachings of all the religions of the world. A Master of different types of Yoga, Paramahamsa Hariharananda was a unique spiritual preceptor. Through the example of his own simple lifestyle filled with love, he taught the scientific technique of Kriya Yoga in theory and in practice. Author of many books, his works have been translated into many Indian and Western languages.

There is no doubt that through his grace and that of his direct disciples, the divine will of Babaji has been and will be fulfilled. He had a charming personality, he could be a playful child, a curious youth or the embodiment of peace and wisdom. He was loving, caring and affectionate and was never distant or rigid. Being the incarnation of love, compassion and service. His life is an ideal of sacrifice and God-consciousness.

At every moment Baba Hariharananda used to teach in countless ways in order to inspire his followers to progress on the spiritual path and his very breath was spent in union with God for the spiritual upliftment of mankind. A unique world teacher, proficient in many languages, free from religious dogma and sectarian beliefs, he has been described as the embodiment of Jesus' love, the clear sightedness of Shankara, the devotion of Shri Chaitanya and the compassion of the Buddha. His spiritual stature is impressive but it was really through his sweet simple smile that one was able to perceive divine bliss.

Baba Hariharananda, as all his disciples lovingly called him all along his lifetime mission has left an indelible imprint in thousands of seekers.

At 6.48 p.m. Eastern Standard Time on December 3, 2002 Paramahamsa Hariharananda peacefully left his mortal body after one final breath. Gurudev exited the body land to immerse himself once more in the supreme almighty Lord. Traditional Vedic last rites were performed the next morning. Hariharanandaji's mortal body remained in his Homestead, Florida, U.S. ashram for one week so his disciples could have a final darshan with the breathless Master.

On the 10th of December 2002 the mortal body of Paramahamsa Hariharananda left the Florida ashram homeward bound for the distant shores of Mother India to be laid to rest with his forefathers.

At Bhubaneswar, Orissa on the 14th of December, he received the state guard of honor, an honor never before bestowed on a monk. On that day, thousands waited to pay tribute to Baba in Hariharananda Gurukulam, Balighai, his final resting place. The mahasamadhi ceremony commenced at 12.30 p.m. on the 15th of December 2002 with many distinguished monks, guests, state officials, and devotees present. Baba was buried with traditional Vedic monastic burial rites. To complete the ceremony, a Shiva lingam named Harihareshwara was installed in the samadhi shrine, a symbol of Baba's union with the Divine.

On the day of the full moon, the 18th of December, more than 200 monks and sadhus from many traditions gathered to offer prayers. Realized Masters are eternally present through their teachings. Anyone who prays or meditates can feel the Masters' presence all along their spiritual journey. Gurudev has promised to help sincere seekers at the time of their need.

DIVINE TEACHINGS OF
PARAMAHAMSA HARIHARANANDA

Breath-control is self-control. Breath-mastery is self-mastery.
Breathlessness stage is deathlessness stage.

If you always watch Him at the top of your head, you will always
feel that you are the living power of God.

Mistakes are made for correction. Illusion leads to disillusion.

God is changing your cells, your atoms, your tissues and your
diaphragm at every moment, you should strive to change your negative
qualities.

Good company will make you good, and bad company will make you
bad. All evils; such as anger, pride, viciousness, cruelty, insincerity,
suspicion, doubt and jealousy are considered bad company.

Opportunity should not be neglected for it may never return.

If your gross "I" will not die, you cannot perceive your real "I".

Every inhalation is a birth. Every exhalation is a death. So one breath is an entire life.

Stay calm, but active and remain compassionately detached.

If you convince yourself that you are not the doer, but your soul is the sole doer, then you will get constant liberation.

When your breath becomes very feeble, then you are really practising Kriya. You are established in truth.

Be still and know that you are the living power of God.

You are to watch the light, sound and vibration all the time to attain liberation.

The needle of the compass of your mind should always point North, towards His domain.

If your soul did not inhale, you would die, it is only because your soul is breathing that you are alive.

Your tongue is more powerful and dangerous than a gun. A gun can kill a person in one shot; but a hurtful word will keep giving pain again and again.

What comes out from your mouth is the talk of God.

You are to reach God in two steps, kri and ya. Remain concentrated at the top and observe your own work from morning till you go to bed.

Every religion teaches the formlessness of God. Kriya Yoga teaches how you can reach that formless stage.

If you do not prepare your field adequately, then you cannot get a good harvest. Similarly, if you do not prepare your body and mind sufficiently through meditation, then you cannot get inner peace.

Always remember that you are God in a human being and a human being in God.

Many chant, sing and dance, even too loudly as if God was deaf. God is all-pervading. He is within you. Without Him you cannot talk. So meditate and realize Him.

There are many mines, but not in every mine will you find a diamond. There are many forests, but not in every forest will you find a sandalwood tree. There are many monks, but a true realized monk who has penetrated beyond nature's splendours, who is free from all bodily senses and worldly attachments, who has reached the introvert stage and who has penetrated the veil behind all religions is extremely rare.

The spine is the principal part of the body. By magnetizing the spine, you will feel divine energy, which in turn hastens your physical, mental, intellectual and spiritual evolution.

Constantly feel that you are not you, you are the real you.

Anger is the greatest enemy of man.

Your five sense organs are your enemies.

Constantly watch the source of all things. Then you will realize that all thoughts come from Him.

As long as you have not cleansed your heart from all impurities, you cannot love. So you are to cleanse your heart and mind through the technique of meditation.

Many thoughts and impressions are stored in the midbrain. You are to erase them through the technique of meditation.

Watch Him day and night in your every thought, word and action. Constant alertness is necessary, if you do this you will have positive and quick results.

Offer everything, including your breath, to God.

Man alone can fully realize God, because his body and mind are so constituted that, in accordance with his desire, man can ascend to a higher plane or descend to a lower stratum of evolution.

Hamsa, or the union of the body (ham) with the soul (sa) keeps a person alive.

Suppose you want to cross a river. If you put one foot in one boat and the other foot in another boat, no doubt the boats will reach the shore, but you will be drowned for sure.

Leave emotion and be motionless.

When someone touches the feet of the guru, he will receive his divine energy.

When imagination stops, realization starts.

Meditation is beyond imagination, hallucination and speculation.

If you want self-realization you do not need to renounce anything, but only to perceive the soul in everything.

If while you work you feel that work is worship and the material world is the living presence of God, you will get liberation.

Due to ignorance, you are constantly merged in illusion, delusion and error and you do not realize that the Creator is abiding in the entire creation.

In order to be realized, you require four things (4 S'); shraddha (deep desire for spirituality), sadhusanga (company of the spiritual Master), sadhana (spiritual practice) and siddhi (perfection).

If someone examines closely the world around him, he will perceive that everything is the play of the soul.

Hatred towards another is felt because of self-interest or because one feels separate or left out, but when a person realizes that he is a part of the multiplicity of the Divine Being, there is no more question of hatred for all are one soul.

Man is born only for self-realization.

Only the realized soul can show the divine path and convert the extrovert mind into a heaven of peace.

If you feel heat, you surmise that fire is very near. Similarly, if you perceive the divine sound, divine light and divine vibration, you are very near to the power of God.

The soul is the real seer; any external thing is seen with the help of the soul.

When you see a flower, you feel it is only a flower. But why do you not think of it as your soul, without the soul there is no flower.

At every moment we should ask our conscience whether we are advancing towards the divine goal or not.

God has created anger, pride, passion, avarice, greed, delusion, illusion and so many other things for our own evolution.

The soul is the silent witness to the three states of life; the wakeful state, the dream state and the state of deep sleep.

Karma means action, both physical and mental. Every action leaves its impression in the subconscious mind and has either a good or a bad effect on person's life.

The mind is the Lord of the senses, but breath rules the mind. So breath-control will lead you to mind control and liberation.

Food is beauty. Food is energy. Food is strength. Food is vitality. Food is brightness and splendour.
So be very careful while taking food.

Feel your wife or your husband as the power of God. If the living God did not breathe within you, then there would be no wife, no husband and no sexual joy.

The spiritual path is just like the edge of a sharp sword. You are to walk every step very cautiously and carefully.

As is the breath, so is the mind. As is the mind, so is man.

Give as much as you can. The more you give the more you receive.

Bondage or liberation are in your hand.

An ounce of practice is far better than tons of theory.

Paramahamsa Prajnanananda

THE LIVING MASTER

Paramahamsa Prajnanananda, is the disciple and spiritual successor of Paramahamsa Hariharananda. After his Mahasamadhi on 3rd of December 2002, Prajnananandaji has taken on his Master's mission of spreading the ancient and sacred teachings of Kriya Yoga to spiritual aspirants leading and guiding many disciples along the path of realisation. Paramahamsa Hariharananda, long before he made him a monk, had said: "Whatever is started by me, has to be completed by him."

Paramahamsa Prajnanananda was born on the 10th of August 1960 in the village of Pattamundai in Orissa. From an early age he was searching for a spiritual teacher and had always been a sincere seeker of truth. In 1980, while still a student, he met his Master Paramahamsa Hariharananda, who later initiated him into the path of Kriya Yoga. This meeting changed his whole life.

He soon went to live with his master in Karar Ashram in Puri and travelled to and fro from Puri to Rourkela and to Cuttack where he was then teaching as a professor of Economics for 11 years. He was called to Europe in 1994 by Gurudev Hariharanandaji to teach Kriya Yoga there.

Brahmachari Triloki Dash, as he was then known, was initiated into Sannyas by his Master, and became Swami Prajnanananda Giri on the 25th of April 1995. The next day, Paramahamsa Hariharananda sent him again to Europe and then to the USA to teach Kriya Yoga through public lectures, seminars, retreats and meditation classes. On 10th of August 1998, on his 39th birthday, the title of Paramahamsa, the highest title reserved for monks and saints who attain the summit of realization was conferred on him by his master.

He is selflessly sacrificing the silent and secluded life of a monk, to lovingly spreading the path of Kriya Yoga, by ceaselessly travelling around the world. The power of his teachings lies in their simplicity and direct relevance to our daily lives. His clear and concise explanations on all the ancient Holy Scriptures and the depth of his metaphorical interpretations are unique. Using Kriya Yoga as a reference point and interpretative tool, Prajnananandaji reveals the hidden truths contained in the most complex passages of the Sacred Texts of the East and West. His vast knowledge and oratory and intellectual skills are fully utilized in interpreting deep philosophical thoughts in the light of modern science and psychology.

Paramahamsa Prajnanananda, in essence, teaches only one lesson: the lesson of love. He urges and directs aspirants on the spiritual path to realize they are all Divine and that one can reach that Super Conscious, blissful state through constant breath-awareness. He is an ocean of wisdom and, being fully grounded within, he can focus on ten tasks at a time with perfect precision and mastery, yet, around him, one always perceives a loving, peaceful yet forceful and joyful energy, the mark of a master who has mastered Himself. Paramahamsa Prajnanananda's life is his message. Once we have offered ourselves to the Lord, the world naturally prostrates at our feet, once we have conquered our mind, we have conquered the world and, once we are successful within, also worldly accomplishments are gained. Once we surrender our own desires to the Lord, we are free from our own personal whims and ambitions and the Divine Will itself becomes our own desire. Once one has found bliss and harmony within, the whole world becomes infused with beauty and joy.

He himself sets an example to one and all on how to realize the connection between ourselves and the Divine; how to surrender and unfold our infinite potential to its fullest, in order to become or be anything we wish, without losing sight of the highest goal in life, thus encouraging his disciples to follow his exemplary life and his teachings with enthusiasm and faith.

Paramahamsa Prajnanananda founded an Ashram at Cuttack in the year 1993 which was renamed as   Prajnana Mission in 1999 on the advice and divine guidance of Paramahamsa Hariharananda. Prajnana Mission has ashrams in Cuttack and in Balighai near Puri in

Orissa. Through the Mission the discipline of Kriya Yoga is taught to sincere seekers irrespective of caste, creed, sex and religion. Prajnana Mission is also dedicated to the service of humanity through many charitable and educational activities.

Balighai Ashram has just been enlarged for intensive retreats, brahmachari courses and seminars. In 1995 Paramahamsa Hariharananda had a dream where Shriyuketshwar directed him to transfer this property to Paramahamsa Prajnanananda predicting that this beautiful ashram will become a place of international reputation where many people would come to stay and meditate.

By Editor

DIVINE TEACHINGS
OF PARAMAHAMSA PRAJNANANANDA

When you pray it is you talking to God
while in meditation it is God talking to you.

Once you have accepted life as a drama, accept it.
if the dream is realized as such,
then the world is done with.

Life is for progress and evolution
and one should listen to the promptings of God
with rapt attention in order not to get into problems.

Past lives influence this present lifetime
and this present life influences the future.
So, be careful today
and spend every moment in God consciousness.

Once formed, a habit becomes powerful,
so powerful that it is difficult to overcome.
To change a habit one has to change one's outlook.

To attain eternal happiness one has to go inside.

Without the power of the soul a body is
as useless as a bulb
when there is no electricity.

The mind is in between the body and the soul
preventing us to perceive the soul.

The soul is ever free and never in bondage.

The true Guru is one who has mastered
his body, senses and mind.

A true Guru is humble, always God conscious
always ready to forgive and guide
with love and compassion.

A Guru is the Master who has realized Truth
following a yogic path
and has obtained the pulse and breathless state
of nirvikalpa samadhi.

Although teachers may be many, Masters are few.

Love and meditation are inseparable.

A Master is one who has thorough control over his mind,
breathing system and, consequently,
over all the systems in his body.
He is one who is simultaneously and constantly
conscious of his inner self and God.

Seeking and perceiving one's own divinity
by practicing a technique,
does not go against any religious belief.

One must constantly endeavour to be perfect
in every thought, word and action.

One reaches the state of perfection through
regular practice and integrated awareness.

When the wave merges back into the ocean
becoming one with the ocean,
it will attain perfection.

Meditation is a silent prayer

The wave is born in the ocean,
but due to temporary delusion it thinks:
"I am the wave."
This 'wave consciousness' brings a sense
of separation from the ocean of Divinity.

When there is only constant perception of unity,
Love will not only manifest towards God, the ocean,
but towards all the other waves.

Prayer is the expression of one's love for God
through the senses
while in meditation all the senses are introvert.

Meditation is the way to attain balance,
inner peace and calmness.

One has to choose the practice that gives
peace and calmness
and makes one's mind more focused.

Your own breath is God.
Use breath in a scientific way.

In order to perceive the light of the soul
and listen to the primordial sound,
no other belief
nor no other preparation is needed
than to close one's eyes and close one's ears.

If you know who you are,
you will be able to live in this world
in a totally different way.

PARAMAHAMSA PRAJNANANANDA
DISPELLS DISCIPLES' DOUBTS

Disciple: *I have come to meet you and understand if I am to request Kriya Yoga initiation from you. I have some questions, may I ask some clarifications on some uncertainties I still have?*

Prajnananandaji: I am happy you have come. You are welcome to ask any question you may deem necessary to feel confident.

Disciple: *May I ask if to practice Kriya Yoga direct guidance from a teacher is absolutely necessary and, if so, what should be our attitude?*

Prajnananandaji: Just as you need a teacher in addition to text books to learn, it is good to practice Kriya Yoga under the direct guidance of a teacher. The Guru disciple relationship is a very special one and a very crucial one too. The Guru disciple relationship is a spiritual and divine relationship, not a material or a business one.

We all believe ourselves to be very intelligent and that we know everything. If you know everything there is no need to go to a Guru. If you go to a Guru to learn something, then be humble. The correct attitude, when you approach a Guru, is to be like a student eager to learn and very receptive. People with real wisdom and love are humble just as a tree loaded with fruit bends down or as a cloud pours down the water it is bearing. Humility is an egoless state.

In the old days, following Indian spiritual tradition, students and teacher used to live together, either always or at least for four months during monsoon period – *chaturmasi*. The ashram where they lived together was called Gurukulam. The disciple was serving his teacher physically and the teacher was serving his disciples intellectually, spiritually and morally. Both were serving each other and the disciple, by observing the Guru, learnt through His example. Nowadays these circumstances are rare as nobody has time. The students don't have time and teachers don't have much time either.

Disciple: *Isn't intellectual understanding sufficient?*

Prajnananandaji: No. It is not enough. You have to meditate and practice what you have understood. Getting a degree in medicine is not enough to become a good doctor. One has to work hard to be successful; without your own effort nothing can be achieved.

In the Kathopanishad I:II:23 it is said:

This Atman cannot be attained by mere study of the scriptures, by intelligence alone or by simply listening to lectures. Through your meditation you will find there is no play of mind or everything is the play of yourself, that when you'll be talking to someone you are talking to yourself and when you are looking at somebody you are looking at yourself. This needs practice. Through practice all is possible.

Disciple: *How to choose a Guru? What are the qualities to identify Him?*

Prajnananandaji: In all the scriptures it is repeatedly stressed to be very careful, selective and scrutinizing in accepting a Master, a Guru. One should watch Him day and night before deciding. Be very careful, as nowadays there is an abundance of false prophets, wolves that may come to you under the pretence of being sheep. Many simply pretend to be masters and are always engaged in a lot of outward show. To be a master is a state of spiritual attainment. When you are to decide, give importance to these basic qualities: a real master has mastered the lower self and is merged in the Supreme Self. The Guru, the Master, is one who has mastered His body, senses and mind. A true Guru is humble, always God conscious, always ready to forgive and guide the disciple along the divine path with love and compassion.

Disciple: *What is the difference between Master, Guru, Swami and Acharyas?"*

Prajnananandaji: Swami is the term to address a monk. A Swami may be a Master, a teacher or a student. Guru in Sanskrit means: "One who is a realized Master". A Guru is the Master who has realized Truth following a yogic path and has obtained the pulse and breathless state of nirvikalpa samadhi. A Master is one who has thorough control over His mind, breathing system and, consequently, over all the systems in His body. He is one who is simultaneously and constantly conscious of His inner self and God. In Indian culture we have Gurus and Acharyas. An Acharya is a teacher and a Guru is the Master, the realized one. So, although teachers may be many, Masters are few.

Disciple: *Can one have more than one teacher? Will Kriya Yoga be in conflict with any of my present spiritual practices or beliefs?*

Prajnananandaji: There are many types of restaurants where Italian or Chinese or Greek food is served. You must have tasted so many varieties of food in your lifetime and all these different tastes are stored in your memory. Now you have decided to try one more restaurant and another type of food! If you are happy with your practice, continue your own practice, but if you are not, come and learn Kriya Yoga. It is not in conflict with any other technique you have been practicing up to now. You can continue to love your teachers or any previous technique you have learnt so far. If it is not out of mere curiosity, come, test and compare. Kriya Yoga has nothing to do with religions. Religions are many, Truth is one. Whether one is a Muslim, a Catholic or a Hebrew one can practice Kriya Yoga, one does not have to be a Hindu to learn Kriya Yoga. The ultimate goal of all practices is one and the same. Seeking and perceiving one's own divinity does not go against any belief.

As far as having more than one teacher one can look at Krishna's life: to teach and show the world the importance and the role of a Guru in one's life Krishna, Himself an incarnation, studied under three Gurus during three different stages of His life. His first Guru was Gargacarya, the family priest, who performed Krishna's thread ceremony – upanayana – and initiated Him into the Gayatri mantra. With this ceremony a Guru starts a disciple on the path of spiritual life. (The sacred thread will remind the disciple of the vows taken of following a disciplined life.) Then Krishna went to Sandipani. In Sanskrit the name Sandipani means one who can kindle the light of knowledge in another person through the energy of his own self-knowledge. Krishna lived in Sandipani's house serving him and learning from him the Vedas, the art of warfare and politics. Krishna's third Guru was Ghora Anghirasa who taught Him Yoga and meditation.

Disciple: *I am a catholic. Will you please explain if Jesus was practicing Kriya?*

Prajnananandaji: Whatever meditation Jesus practiced must have been very similar to Kriya because Jesus' teachings and what we experience practicing Kriya Yoga are very similar. Love Jesus and meditate. In spiritual life, if you are really sincere, God will teach you through different media. The teaching is far more important than the medium so, if you want, drink the wine but do not hold on to the bottle. Teachers are like bottles of wine: drink the wine and then throw the bottle away!

Disciple: *Was Jesus realized?*

Prajnananandaji: Jesus does not require my certification. Jesus was, is and always will be. Love Jesus and practice meditation.

Disciple: *What is meant by Christ-consciousness?*

Prajnananandaji: Christ is the symbol of eternal perfection. Christ is

Truth and the Path to perfection. One has to tread the path of perfection in order to reach the state of soul consciousness and Christ-consciousness. One must constantly endeavour to be perfect in every thought, word and action. One reaches the state of perfection through regular practice and integrated awareness. When the wave merges back into the ocean becoming one with the ocean, it will attain perfection. The wave is born in the ocean, but due to temporary delusion it thinks: "I am the wave." This 'wave-consciousness' brings a sense of separation from the ocean and, due to this, many complexities appear in one's life. When the wave fully perceives that it is an integral part of the ocean, the ego and delusion will disappear. Only constant perception of unity will remain and, as a consequence, love will manifest towards not only the ocean, but towards all the other waves. This is why, at a certain point, Jesus said: "I and the Father are one."

Disciple: *What is the difference between prayer and meditation?*

Prajnananandaji: When you pray it is you talking to God, while in meditation it is God talking to you. In meditation you close your eyes to feel the presence of God within you. Love and meditation are inseparable. While praying you look at an image or any symbol, you sing the glory of God and you talk to God, therefore you use your senses, while meditation is a silent prayer; you close your eyes, your ears and your mouth to perceive the otherwise inaudible talk of God. When you pray you talk to God while in meditation you listen to God talking to you. Those who meditate go into the inner chambers of silence and listen to the melodious sound of Om or Amen, the on-going primeval sound. When you pray your eyes are open, so you see the sunlight or the moonlight, but during meditation, through your third eye, you perceive the light of the soul. Prayer is the expression of one's love for God through the senses while meditation is a silent prayer and the senses are introvert.

Disciple: *What will change in my life if I start meditating?*

Prajnananandaji: Meditation will bring completeness in your life. Everybody wants to be happy and healthy. Everybody wants love and understanding in one's life. With balance and calmness you can attain all this. Meditation is the way to attain balance, inner peace and calmness in whatever circumstance one may find oneself in.

WHEN DOUBTS CONTINUE

Disciple: *I was initiated some years ago, but I did not practice. I then started practicing another technique which entails deconcentration of the mind. May I also practice Kriya Yoga which entails concentration? Are they compatible?*

Prajnananandaji: You are in a spiritual crisis. You have created your own confusion. You are responsible and you have to solve it. From my young age I have met many monks, I went to many ashrams, and even now I go; I loved them all and learnt a lot from them. In my spiritual life I am particularly indebted to Ramakrishna Paramahamsa, Swami Sivananda of the Divine Life Society, Swami Nigamananda Paramahamsa and Swami Swarupananda Paramahamsa. Apart from my Guru these four great spiritual Masters have influenced my spiritual growth and I still love their teachings even if they are not in the body any longer. Meeting with many saints, having their darshan, observing their behaviour and being in their presence has taught me so much. For example if any of you have met Swami Chidananda Saraswati you must have been touched by his remarkable humbleness and simplicity and you may have felt how powerfully elevating it is to be in his presence. So, to be in the presence and listen to great masters is not wrong, but as far as initiation is concerned, it is a totally different matter. People, especially in the West, go here and there and it is not advisable. In spiritual life it is better to follow one Guru without seeking here and there. Gurudev, in such cases, often used to answer: "Write to your own Guru and get permission." When seekers ask me, I always encourage them not to change and to continue with their practice if happy with it. One has to choose the practice that gives peace and calmness and makes one's mind more focused. One should also take into consideration where one receives more support in clearing one's doubts.

Disciple: *Can one practice Kriya Yoga without faith in God?*

Prajnananandaji: In order to perceive the light of the soul and listen to the primordial sound, no other belief nor no other preparation is needed than to close one's eyes and close one's ears. Faith in a personal God is not necessary. Your own breath is God. If breath stops, there is no life. You cannot deny this, can you? Use breath in a scientific way. Lahiri Mahasaya often used to say: " My way of worship is not the usual one. I do not need any Ganga water, neither flowers nor utensils for my worship, nor do I burn incense or light lamps. I have forgotten who Shiva, Kali or Durga are. I am merged in myself."

To meditate, one does not need to follow any religion, nor any new external type of worship. In order to perceive the light of the soul and listen to the primordial sound, no other belief nor no other preparation is needed than to close one's eyes and close one's ears.

Disciple: *Is it really necessary to know who I am?*

Prajnananandaji: If you know who you are, you will be able to live in this world in a totally different way. Life will become really sacred and beautiful. You will still be in the world, but you will know what is the role you are to play and, therefore, you will play your role better. To illustrate this I will tell you a story. A king, after his lunch, went to take a nap. In his sleep he dreamt that he was a beggar and that, as he was extremely hungry, he was going from door to door begging for food. When he woke up from his dream the king started saying: I am hungry, give me some food. The king's attendants were all very surprised as he had had his lunch only a few minutes before, but the king insisted that he was hungry and that he had not had food for three days. At everyone's dismay he acted as a beggar and told his attendants he had been knocking at so many doors, but nobody had given him food. For quite some time his attendants had to go on telling him he was a king and not a beggar and that he had just finished his lunch. When the king woke up completely, he felt so puzzled and asked himself many times: "Who am I, really? In the dream I was a beggar and I was experiencing hunger. As a king I have just had my food and I am not hungry. Am I the king or the beggar?" When he realized and was conscious of being the king he went to his Guru to ask him who he really was and the Guru told him he was neither the beggar nor the king. The beautiful dialogue between king Janaka and his Guru, Astavakra constitutes an enlightening book: *The Astavakra Gita*.

If you know who you are, if you know why you have come to this world and where you are going you will have fulfilled the purpose of your life.

Disciple: *How long will it take to know who I am?*

Prajnananandaji: Spiritual experience is not a degree or a diploma. When words and the world disappear, then you will experience the play of consciousness everywhere. One may take a very short time and others a longer time.

Disciple: *How will I know I've made it?*

Prajnananandaji: Slowly experience will come. You will know through your own meditation. You are the only best judge, but for the time being practice more and meditate each day a little more. When a child is at primary school, if the teacher says this letter is 'A', the child accepts it and practices it. Book learning and scholarship alone do not give self-realization.

Disciple: *I do realize it is getting rather late, but please clarify also why is Kriya Yoga said to be scientific?*

Prajnananandaji: Scientific truths are verifiable. If I tell you that there is electricity in the wire, is it a belief or a truth? It is scientifically true as you can verify yourself. Scientific truths are verifiable. Your experience will be the same as any other person's experience under similar conditions. This is what happens in Kriya Yoga. All those who come for initiation and those who practice the techniques, from the very first day, see the light and listen to sound. It is scientific. The theory and practice of Kriya Yoga is not a mere belief, it is truth. Through breath control we can control the entire system, even our thinking process. When one practices Kriya Yoga, each and every internal organ is massaged and energized. It is scientific. Through the practice of Kriya one provides more oxygen to the brain in a scientific way. Oxygen is the nutrition of the brain. Spiritual life is not based on belief, it is direct experience. Now go to your room as it is late and you may come again for a few more questions before you leave.

ABOUT THE MONKEY MIND

Disciple: *Thank you for the beautiful initiation ceremony, I tried to practice but, as soon as I sat on the floor, my mind started chatting even more loudly. What should I do?"*

Prajnananandaji: It is not the body that comes with you life after life, but the mind. Lfe after life you have kept the mind in an extrovert state. Even in this lifetime, since childhood and for years and years, you have kept your mind untrained, restless and in an extrovert state. It is only since a few hours that you are trying to discipline the mind and keep it under control. Previously you always followed the command and the whims of the mind and now, by simply sitting down on the floor, you pretend and expect to have a silent peaceful mind! Please have a little patience!!

The mind is a bundle of thoughts. Let thoughts come, watch them, but do not entertain them. If you welcome a thought it will give rise to a chain of related thoughts. Avoid those thoughts that can be avoided. Watch your thoughts, but do not welcome them. By avoiding repeatedly a thought, the thought will die away.

Disciple *I had never realized that I had such a disobedient mind. it is worse than a mad monkey. Will also my mind calm down?*

Prajnananandaji: The mind is mischievous. As soon as you try to discipline your mind, the mind starts a non-cooperating movement to maintain its independence.

At the beginning a conscious person also has to recognize his weaknesses and negativities. Transformation is in itself progress. Knowing one's weaknesses is strength. If thoughts come, just watch them and, instead of trying to control them try and change their quality.

Disciple: *How do we change the quality of our thoughts and get more loving and divine thoughts?*

Prajnananandaji: To change the quality of your thoughts be very regular in your meditation practice, choose good company and read spiritual books. This will help you to create new and positive thoughts. Writing down a spiritual teaching and contemplating on it is also very useful. One should also try and change the quantity of thoughts. Through regular meditation one should reduce from ten thoughts per minute to six thoughts and then come down to two per minute and finally, during concentration, only one thought. Meditation is a thoughtless state. Breath control is mind control. Practice and be patient.

ABOUT GROSS, SUBTLE AND CAUSAL BODY

Disciple: *Where do thoughts come from?*

Prajnananandaji: "Thoughts come from memory, from one's subtle body, which is the storehouse of memory. The subtle body is the memory bank."

Disciple: *Wait a second please! I did not know where thoughts came from, but if I do not know about having a subtle body, then I will really get muddled! What is the subtle body?"*

Prajnananandaji: Very few people realize that rather than one body, we actually have three: the gross body, or physical body, to which we are so inordinately attached, the astral body or subtle body that can be defined as a person's mental makeup or personality and the causal body that is composed of our ignorance and knowledge. The gross body changes continuously, old cells die and new ones form in an endless cycle, but one day the gross body will perish. The gross body is composed of the five elements. The subtle body, also known as astral body, contains the imprint of all our various tendencies, samskaras, formed by repeated experiences, thought patterns and past lives' actions. The subtle body can be described as the combination of senses, vital breaths and experiences had through the mind and intellect. These constitute our own unique personality that distinguishes us from any other person. The subtle body is much larger than the gross body since it encompasses the mind. While the gross body is limited in its activities, with the mind one can travel anywhere at lightening speed. Most of us are unable to use the astral body to its full capacity. The astral body is at its most effective capacity when the mind is pure, clean and concentrated. The immense spiritual energy that lies hidden and untapped in the subtle body, if properly used, will enable us to experience inexplicable joy and bliss. The causal body can be defined as the body of ignorance as well as knowledge. When in the state of complete ignorance and self absorption, ignorance covers our other two bodies and therefore is the primary cause for our continuous cycle of births, deaths and suffering. Once ignorance is eliminated we are liberated, free from bondage.

Ordinary worldly knowledge cannot remove this body of ignorance. It is only self-knowledge born of deep analysis and perception that leads us to true liberation. The Vedas teach that only when we transcend all the three bodies we can realize the Absolute."

Disciple: *How does one arrive at a blissful state?*

Prajnananandaji: I'll tell you a story. A man was walking down the street and on his way he found a dazzling stone, which looked precious.

It was such a valuable stone that overnight he became very rich. From that day onwards, while he was walking, he kept his eyes glued to the ground in the hope of finding another stone as valuable as the previous one. Years went by and, when already rather old, he saw another dazzling stone, so he picked it up, but only to realize that it was a broken glass reflecting the brilliance of the sun above. Surprised he looked up and saw a beautiful bright sun. He had never seen anything that beautiful. So he threw away the piece of glass and, from that day onwards, started looking up. In human life, even if we sometimes have to look down, we should remember to look up. Tapping the source of bliss is possible if one can stop the play of the mind. The mind is the cause of trouble. The mind, once regulated and trained can be a good friend, a supportive pillar in life. A concentrated mind is the medium needed to achieve the goal of self-realization. We are born in bliss, live in bliss and merge in bliss. One attains this blissful state tapping the source, in the cave of the cranium, near the fontanel. This is the inexhaustible and unending source of perfect and infinite joy. By exploring the chakras and spending some time each day stilling our active mind, shutting down our overactive senses and listening quietly to the pranava, the divine sound, we can tap the source within and attain unending bliss.

THE GOAL

Disciple: *What should our goal in life be?*

Prajnananandaji: Yogis say it is Nirvikalpa samadhi.

Jnanis say it is the state of turiya.

Bhaktas say it is to be always in love with God.

There are four stages of evolution:

1) When one crosses Brahma-granthi, one attains control over the lower three centers and one sees God's presence everywhere..

2) When one crosses Vishnu-granthi, one reaches the stage of salokya and, whether keeping one's eyes closed or open, one only perceives God's presence and light everywhere.

3) When one penetrates Rudra-granthi one attains constant union with the Divine

4) When one goes even beyond, it is the state of nirvikalpa samadhi, nirvana or turiya, which are one and the same. One who attains this state is free from all inward attachments and lives in the world as a free soul.

Perfection is the path, perfection is Truth and perfection is the goal.

Disciple: *What should we change in our daily life to reach the goal?*

Prajnananandaji: In order to fulfill the goal of life, one must take note of one's weaknesses and failures through earnest self analysis and, with the utmost honesty, fight to eliminate all the negative impulses from one's life. Every evening one should contemplate and evaluate one's activities throughout the day and have the strong determination not to commit the same mistake over and over again. Mistakes are to be corrected, repeating the same mistake becomes a bad habit and, as once a bad habit is ingrained it becomes difficult to eliminate it, one should strive to live a disciplined life becoming regular and systematic in one's daily routine. A disciplined life is the barometer of the fulfillment of one's sadhana. Success is perfection and perfection is success in one's efforts. To achieve the highest goal in life one should possess sufficient physical, mental, emotional and spiritual strength in order to overcome all the obstacles. The spiritual path is said to be like a razor's edge, it is very difficult and at the same time very easy. One should learn to use time in an economical way; just as some people become misers with money, one should become a miser about spending one's time. Time is more precious than money. Discipline, ingrained good habits and a careful use of time will help us regulate both body and mind. A yogi always does everything with adequate measure and always at the proper time. One succeeds in attaining the highest goal of life if one has inner strength. The desire to transform one's life should lead one to set up a goal-oriented life filled with a combination of prayer and love for the Divine and His entire creation.

Disciple: *Is samadhi the end and the goal?*

Prajnananandaji: Spirituality is endless and continuous. In the Autobiography of a Yogi, when Sriyukteshwar resurrected in front of Yoganandaji while he was in a hotel in Bombay, he said he was meditating in another plane of existence where many other evolved souls also existed. As God is infinite so is spiritual life.

YOGA

Disciple: *What does Yoga actually mean?*

Prajnananandaji: Yoga in Sanskrit has innumerable meanings, but in the spiritual context yoga means:

Self-control
Union

One who leads a life of self-control attains immortality. Yoga means to discipline oneself with love, out of one's own choice, in order to improve one's body, mind and thoughts and to shape one's life always aiming at perfection. This is self-control.

Yoga is union of the body and soul. Yoga means realizing 'I am the soul in the body' This union is Yoga and it is achieved through the help of breath. After this step, one has to realize the union of the individual soul with the Supreme Self. Yoga is to understand the relationship between oneself and the Supreme Self.

Yoga means perceiving constant unity with the Almighty in every breath. If one feels constantly united with the Lord like the wave and the ocean, one attains balance. The ocean and the wave are inseparable. If one thinks and experiences: 'I am the wave and God is the ocean of cosmic consciousness and I am united with the ocean, God, one will reach a state of permanent peace'.

Disciple: *You tell us to love our breath. How do I love my breath?*

Prajnananandaji: What is love? When you love someone you want to be near to that person, don't you? When you love, you want to see the beloved one and listen to his or her words. So this means you want to be close to someone you love. To love your breath just close your eyes and watch how the air goes in and out while you are breathing. Practice this rhythmic breathing technique keeping inhalation and exhalation equal and you will become more peaceful. If you want to meditate, you should arrive at the point when there is no air coming out of your nostrils. There will still be inhalation and exhalation, but no warm breath will be coming out of your nose. By making your breath rhythmic you become conscious of your breath. This is a very simple technique that will soothe your mind, will enable you to relax and attain God consciousness.

LOVE AND FAMILY LIFE

Disciple: *What is the difference between ordinary love and divine love?*

Prajnananandaji: God's love is eternal, pure, divine and without expectations. What you call ordinary love is not love, it is business. You invest something expecting a return.

Real love is a perception of inner fulfillment and distributing your fulfillment to others without any further expectation.

Disciple: *How am I to balance spiritual life and family life?*

Prajnananandaji: Do not divide life into spiritual life and family life. Our entire life is spiritual. Spirituality is a life of love. First love yourself and know what the self or soul is. If you do not know how to love yourself, then you cannot love others; if there is no love in you, you cannot give love to others. Remember unhappiness and depression are contagious in a family. Each person vents out their frustrations on others. Just as anger is contagious, love is also contagious. Think of yourself as a monk living in the family and lead a life of understanding. Prepare and serve food as though cooking and serving food to God.

Food cooked with agitation or worry will carry those same vibrations and these vibrations will affect all those who partake of it. If you are joyful and strong, you can make others happy. Love your breath, breath is your life.

You will remain in an undisturbed state of peace and joy if, while leading a family life with your wife and children, you are conscious of your breath; be conscious of your breath even while working in the office.

Householders should practice moderation in all their sense enjoyments though, while living in a society, one cannot abstain from them totally, one can be moderate. You will have to face many temptations living in today's society; take it as a test of your strength.

Desires are like fire. However much fuel you add to the fire, it keeps consuming the fuel and never says no. Control the amount of fuel and live in moderation. When problems come, tune your mind to Divinity, pray and meditate. Meditate every day without neglecting your household duties. A householder's life is not easy, but it is possible to lead a perfect, peaceful and joyful householder's life if one has real love as love can change anything; follow the script of the divine drama and play the role God has allotted to you in the best possible way. In the Bhagavad Gita VI:17 Krishna says:

> *'yuktahara viharasya yukta cestasya karmasu*
> *yukta svapnavabodhasya yogo bhavati duhkhaha'*

> (With moderation in food, in your activities, in all
> your efforts, in sleep and in the wakeful state, Yoga
> will remove all the suffering from your life.)

Disciple: *What are the four stages of life as per the Sacred Scriptures?*

Prajnananandaji: The first stage of life is when one has to study and learn self-control and moral discipline.

The second stage includes marriage, social life, work and children.

The third stage is when the children reach the age of twenty. Then one should start detaching from them. One should now start using one's skills and talents for the good of humanity as seva and not to earn money.

The fourth stage is when one should set aside more time for meditation living in a hermitage or a monastery leading a life of renunciation, as sannyasis do.

Disciple: *Which are the first teachings we can share with our own children when they are still not old enough for initiation, and how to communicate better with them?*

Prajnananandaji: You can teach them some deep breathing and you can teach them to bow. Bowing and touching the feet, kneeling down, or a whole body prostration is a good principle.

Disciple: *By the way, what is the reason why we touch the feet of a spiritual person?*

Prajnananandaji: When one touches the feet of a spiritual person, his spiritual energy flows into the person who is bowing. Teach the children to bow to God, to parents and to the elders. Pray for a minute before taking food, explaining to the children why you pray. Discipline children with love, do not communicate with agitation nor with a cross face or the children will avoid you. Silence is the best communication. Parents tend to have expectations: the yogic method is to do your best and accept the result.

Disciple: *Can you please teach me how to avoid discussions in the family and in particular between husband and wife?*

Prajnananandaji; When these critical situations occur you should ask yourself if by being upset or angry it helps to solve the problem. Agitation will only increase the problem. Sit and meditate, practice the bow. Watch your thoughts or practice deep breathing. In these cases people tend to react, but it would be far better to analyze why the disagreement has happened and how one can solve it. If you are not strong enough to find a solution through your prayers or positive understanding, stay away from the problem for a while. Do not react immediately as an immediate reaction is never a rational reaction. Forgiveness is strength and only a strong person can forgive. Always be inwardly aware that it is all only a drama and play your role well, without ever attempting to reform and change others. In this drama of life we find ourselves in difficulties because we do not listen to the promptings of the Supreme Director, God, and therefore we start our own 'dialogues' which eventually cause a lot of suffering. Lead a life of love and understanding, love gives and forgives. Create your rhythms of meditating regularly, be peaceful and divine.

Disciple: *Is it bad to have some ambition in life?*

Prajnananandaji: Ambition in itself is not bad, but you should pay particular attention to the reason why you may want to have more wealth. For example: there exists a general tendency to believe that if one could afford to buy a house one would be happier. So, as a result, one ends up working day and night for many years till one has enough money to buy a house. When one has earned enough one will buy the new house. Is one happy in the new house? No. People, at this point, generally want someone to share the house with, so they get married. Now that one is married, is one happy? No. Now they want children. As you may see it is a never-ending story. To have ambitions it is not bad, but the real, true ambition should be to experience continuous happiness and inner joy through God consciousness.

COLOUR OF CLOTHES

Disciple: *Baba, I have noticed that most of the people here in the ashram are wearing white clothes. Are white clothes conducive to deeper meditation? Are they a must for a seeker?*

Prajnananandaji: Yoga is a practical lifestyle. Since clothes and the way we dress influence our body and mind, making us self-conscious, we should strive to use simple, comfortable clothing. Some people just pose instead of seriously transforming their life; they merely start wearing only white clothes and applying a red dot between their eyebrows without making a sincere effort to transform their lives. This has nothing to do with meditation nor with spirituality. In spiritual life you are to train your mind. Outer clothing and appearances are not that important. Lahiri Mahasaya once said: 'If ochre robes were a sign of being realized, then are we to consider as realized all the cows with such earth colour hair?' And, when one man who was on the point of becoming a monk asked Lahiri Mahasaya if, as a sannyasi, he had to have matted locks Lahiri Mahasaya pointed out: 'Does the weight of the thread and of matted hair show one is carrying the Lord?'

How can you think that by merely changing the colour of your clothes you can become more spiritual? Do not pose or expose yourself as spiritual; it would be more suitable to hide rather than to expose oneself.

Gurudev used to say: 'Without colouring my mind, if I only colour my clothes it is not real spiritual life.' I was never interested in the colour of clothes, but I simply followed Gurudev's wishes to make Him happy.

I will tell you a story. Once upon a time there was a jackal that used to roam near the house of a washer man. This washer man daily used a special blue liquid to obtain immaculate white clothes. One day the jackal fell into the pot of this blue liquid and came out all blue! He looked so strange that he himself got frightened. Everybody was looking at this strange blue being, everybody asked him who he was and the jackal developed ego at being blue. He started telling himself he was a great jackal, then he started telling others: 'I am the greatest divine being on earth, I am a divine being.' At a certain point he even started pretending the other jackals should give him a massage!!! That was a little too much, so one of the young jackals became a little suspicious and decided to watch him day and night. One day, with the intention of exposing him, the young jackal told all the other jackals to start singing. As they all started singing the blue jackal could not resist it and joined in the singing, thus exposing himself as a jackal rather than a divine being.

CHAKRAS

Disciple: *I heard the term* chakra *for the first time during the initiation. Could you kindly teach me what they are and what role they have in our body and in spiritual practices as I doubt I may not find in the west the exact explanation? How do they really influence our life?*

Prajnananandaji: "The term chakra stands for cerebrospinal centers. You can find all the necessary basic information in the book *The Universe Within*, but for the moment just know that chakras are the potential energy centers with a storehouse of the strength, stability, knowledge and love a person needs. When these centers are seldom used, they rust and become useless. One should learn how to direct the life energy to accelerate one's own spiritual evolution and growth. Each chakra represents certain human qualities and can be the source of endless misery if left uncontrolled and, on the contrary, if one knows how to direct and control that life force one can achieve immeasurable and endless bliss. Instead of running endlessly after the dazzling exterior world, we need to learn how to fix our attention on the magnificence of the universe within. Those seekers who know how to concentrate in the chakras in a steady and informed manner and who regularly meditate on the highest goal of self-realization, will gain steadiness of mind.

We generally speak about the seven main chakras that are located in the spine, from bottom to the top of the head:

Muladhara - also called first center or money center is located at the base of the spine. It represents the earth element and the pleasures through material possessions.

Swadhisthana – also called second center or family center is located in the sacral region. It represents the water element and passion.

Manipura – also known as third center or navel center is located in the navel region. It represents the fire element and it is the food center where we derive our physical energy, our vitality.

Anahata – also called heart center or emotional center. It is located in the dorsal region and represents the air element. It is the seat of our feelings, passions, love and hates, likes and dislikes.

Vishuddha – also called the neck center is the center of creativity and intellect. Music, art, philosophy and theology emerge from this center.

Ajñā – also called soul center is the dwelling place of the third eye, It is located between the eyebrows and is beyond all elements. It is the seat of the soul.

Sahasrara – also called fontanel at the crown of the head. Beyond elements. It is the entryway to the Absolute.

Most of our energy is untapped because rather than looking to the source, we spend our precious time searching for answers outside ourselves. Meditation is the key to unlock the treasures buried deep within us that can transform our life from an ordinary one into an extraordinary one.

Disciple: *What is one to think or visualize while concentrating on the chakras?*

Prajnananandaji: Remember that meditation is not imagination, meditation is direct experience, so there is nothing to think or imagine. When you have an experience, just observe it as the witness. The Lord has given you a field (the body) and if you lovingly and patiently sow the seeds of sadhana in the soil, the crop will be a inestimable and unimaginable treasure. Hidden truths will slowly be revealed to you while you meditate. Close your eyes, shut your senses off and look at the divine crop with your inner eye.

CONCENTRATION AND MEDITATION

Disciple: *Baba, I am back after a year of practicing at home. I realize, now that I meditate here in this ashram, I experience more peace and ananda here than when I meditate at home. Why?*

Prajnananandaji: I am happy to see you again! Do not worry, this does not mean that your Kriya practice is different or wrong when you meditate at home, rather that you have not yet transformed your home into a spiritual home or into an ashram. At home you live with more emotions and more reactions, while here in the ashram, to some extent, you are free from emotions and reactions. The atmosphere changes in places where many people meditate on a regular basis and this is why you find it easier to meditate more deeply in this ashram.

Disciple: *During these past months I read some of your teachings, will you allow me to ask some more questions? I wish you could clarify what is the difference between concentration and meditation?*

Prajnananandaji: Meditate more and you will have less doubts. Concentration is having a single thought and meditation is having no thought.

Disciple: *What are the major obstacles to concentration and meditation?*

Prajnananandaji: When one meditates regularly many negative thoughts will surface just as, when you soak and wash your dirty clothes with water and soap, all the dirt comes out. To obtain perfectly clean clothes one has to rub them vigorously for a while. At the beginning of one's spiritual life many negative thoughts and emotions will surface. But, if instead of getting discouraged, one insists with unwavering regularity in the practice, they will disappear.

Being aware of the main obstacles to concentration and meditation will allow you to recognize and overcome them. I will list these obstacles for you to ponder over:

Disease
Laziness or idleness
Lack of motivation
Doubt
Non rhythmic-breathing
Over eating
Talking too much
Traveling too much
The type of company one keeps
Sleep
Irregularity
Overworking and over-exercising
Expectation
Over confidence
Ego

Concentration is a great asset in one's life and very practical also in everyday life. Through a regulated life style, self control, discipline and meditation one reaches constant inner peace. One will be peaceful both at home with one's family as well as at work and one will be able to maintain such a blissful state even while sleeping and dreaming. Through meditation one can improve the necessary discipline and self-control. Through practice everything becomes possible.

Disciple: *There is a beautiful book written by Gurudev entitled* **Kriya Yoga**, *could you please tell me how Kriya Yoga affects us physically?*

Prajnananandaji: I will give you the information, most willingly: Our brain power and mental receptivity are expanded through Kriya practice. At the same time, as the blood receives more oxygen it gets purified and one's blood circulation in the body improves enormously. Physically one looks healthier and the skin acquires a new light. Through the breathing techniques one not only increases one's life span, but one preserves good health and an alert mind. If the number of breathings per minute is less, our lungs take rest and our life span increases. Normally a person takes about 18 natural inhalations per minute. During the sexual act the respiration is accelerated to 30 inhalations per minute. When one is angry the breathing is even faster: one breathes 34 and 40 times per minute. It is said that an elephant breathes only ten times per minute and that is why it lives for such a long time. Crocodiles and turtles breathe four times per minute and their life span is over a 100 years. During sleep we only breathe ten times per minute and the result is complete rest. When one learns and practices slow-deep breathing, as during sleep, then one will obtain calmness. When sufficient oxygen goes to the lungs, heart and brain, oxygen being the nutrition of the brain, one increases mental power, prompt understanding and quick receptivity. A normal man breathes 15 times in a minute. In Kriya breathing one breath lasts about 15 seconds and, if you practice regularly you can arrive at one breath per minute.

TIME, POSTURE AND WHERE TO MEDITATE

Disciple: *I have had some discussions with some pandits on which is the best time for meditation, can you please set the rule?*

Prajnananandaji: The best time is when you get up from bed in the mornings. At that moment your body is relaxed and the mind is calm. There are four junctions during the day: early morning when the night becomes morning, at midday when the morning becomes afternoon, at sunset when the afternoon becomes night and at night when the evening becomes night. These junctions are considered the best moments to meditate, but anyway, in the end, any moment is good.

Disciple: *Baba, is it also true that one should always try and meditate in a certain place?*

Prajnananandaji: Gurudev used to say that Sri Ramakrishna had stated that there are three places where you should sit for meditation:
1) in the forest,
2) in a corner of one's house
3) in your mind.

In the *Autobiography of a Yogi* there is a story of two friends who went to the Himalayas to retreat and meditate, but as soon as they saw a tiger they ran away frightened and swore never to go back to the Himalayas again. There is no need to go to the forest. What is required is that we live in the shelter of and solitude of an internal forest. Also this forest contains the wild dangerous animals of emotions, anger and pride which need to be substituted by the power of meditation. A quiet corner in your house is the practical answer. Both the forest and the house are simply physical locations and to go to these places sometimes we need time. To go to the natural forest of one's mind is simpler. Make your mind the forest where you can retreat whenever you like, in whatever circumstances and surroundings. The mind is the best place for meditation. Meditate internally. We need to go inward, keeping the mind peaceful and tranquil. Many monks go to the cremation grounds for their meditation. Indian cremation grounds are apt to create detachment due to the incredible smell of burnt bodies! We are all so attached to our body and it does help to sit in a cremation ground for some time as there one can truly witness how this beautiful body is reduced to a pile of ashes in a thrice. In the West you have nicely decorated cemeteries, still the body is a handful of ashes.

Disciple: *In the* **Bhagavad-Gita** *Sri Krishna talks about 'sucau dese', what should we put into practice of His teaching?"*

Prajnananandaji: 'Sucau dese' literally means to sit in a clean, pure and holy place. If your mind is not calm and quiet wherever you happen to sit, you will find it difficult to meditate. In this body temple there is one place that is calm and quiet: in-between the eyebrows and at the top of the head, from the midpoint of the eyebrows to the crown of the head which is known as sahasrara chakra. This space from ajna chakra to sahasrara chakra, said to take up 10 fingers' space, is the real place of calmness or sacau dese.

Disciple: *Is a deer skin necessary for the place where we are to regularly meditate?*

Prajnananandaji: Tantrics even sit on a dead body not yet cremated, a horrible and crude practice! But where is the difference when we sit on a polyester blanket? What is polyester? Nothing more than decomposed matter, a dead product! One should meditate in such a way that there is no sense of the body.....as if the body were dead. In paravasta, we go beyond the body; we do not feel it any longer.

In olden days the rule was that one should prepare three layers to create some insulation from the ground. While meditating, energy is produced and since the earth is a conductor of electricity, it is good to sit on something non-conducting. The three layers were:

A grass carpet (kusa)
A tiger or a deer skin (ajina)
A silk cloth on top. (cela)

The metaphorical meaning of sitting on kusa is: to sit on muladhara. Grass represents the earth and muladhara is the earth center. In Sanskrit *Ajina*, further to skin, also means not easy to control. One should be above the second center, svadhistana chakra, which represents passion and sexuality that is always difficult to control and overcome. Cela (cloth) also means fire. Fire is present in the third center, manipura chakra or navel center. So the perfect asana, to meditate properly, should be to stay above muladhara, svadhistana and manipura. Come up to the cranium, sit there and meditate. The place above the midpoint of the eyebrows is sucau dese. Yogic scriptures have another name for sahasrara, it is brahmarandhra. If one could remain established there even for the fraction of a second one is freed from all sins and attains brahmaloka. Gurudev used to repeat that one was not sitting on the floor, but in fontanel, that even if in the meditation hall there were hundred people meditating, one was alone. To be alone all one had to do was to close one's eyes.

Disciple: *What about the posture? Should one sit in the lotus posture? Which posture helps concentration?*

Prajnananandaji: The external posture is not so important, but it is advisable to keep the spine straight. In Patanjali Yoga Sutra it is suggested to adopt "sthira sukhamasanam" which means the right posture is that in which one is comfortable and one can be still and steady for a longer period of time. Any posture is fine as long as one can forget the presence of the body. Unduly painful positions make us more aware of the body and keep us anchored in its consciousness, hindering our ability to go beyond.

Disciple: *I must confess that sometimes, when I have had a very busy day, my mind goes to the market instead of concentrating. When the mind is not cooperating during meditation, should we continue or stop?*

Prajnananandaji: Continue. Do bows or mahamudra. Even if these seem to be physical exercises, the mind will calm down. If, notwithstanding all this, the mind continues to remain restless, open your eyes and calmly look at a picture you love or chant the names of the Lord. Change the point of meditation, but do not stop. Our mind always tries to test us. When you are trying to keep the mind under control, the mind wants to see if you are really meditating or not and it will suggest some other work to test your desire for meditation. If you get up immediately, the mind will know that your desire for meditation is rather weak. As the mind always tries to pull you down, if you are not determined and disciplined you will give into her whims.

Disciple: *I am a little confused. Please kindly tell us what you think about visions during meditation. Do they have significance? If so, how to understand them?*

Prajnananandaji: There are 2 kinds of visions:
1) People may have hallucinations.
2) It may really be a vision.

How to know the difference? Analyze the state of your mind: if it is calm and quiet the vision could be a real experience. In this case you should also accurately verify and analyze the message it carries, as in reality, a vision containing no message means nothing. Analyze the vision and find out its message. Do not go around asking others about its meaning. Different people may give you various explanations, which may only increase your confusion. The same God who gave you the vision will also give you the wisdom to understand its message.

Disciple: *I would really like to improve and transform my life. Please tell me which are the most important qualities needed by a spiritual seeker?*

Prajnananandaji: For a quick spiritual evolution a seeker needs to acquire the following six qualities:

1) Belief in one's own path and practice.
2) Love and faith in the words of the teacher.
3) Love and respect for the Guru.
4) Balance and equanimity.
5) Control of the senses.
6) Moderation in food.

In the yogic scripture *Siva Samitha* (5-14) we find:
Avoid bad company, live in good company and in every inhalation and exhalation think of God.

Disciple: *How to develop faith in the technique we are practicing?*

Prajnananandaji: You have the example of all the Kriya Masters who followed this same technique and were successful and you have the scriptures attesting to its validity. Believing that the Masters have achieved enlightenment will enable you to achieve the same goal. In life we often have faith and belief in many things without verifying them. When you go to a doctor you believe he has a degree and you accept his advice without asking his certificate. In spirituality belief and faith are important, but do not believe blindly. Have belief, but meditate and experience. The experiences may vary from one person to another, but there will surely be experiences.

Disciple: *How to always be in equanimity and balance avoiding ups and downs?*

Prajnananandaji: When you practice Kriya Yoga, during the bow, you turn right and left. By this practice, in a very subtle way, you gain more and more equanimity and balance. There should be a certain balance between the two lobes of the brain. In the left lobe are stored thoughts and in the right lobe are stored emotions and logic. By balancing these one attains equanimity. Another way to gain a balanced state of mind is to have equal breath in the right and left nostril. When breath is flowing more through the left nostril, there is a tendency to be idle and calm. When breath is flowing more through the right nostril it causes activity and restlessness. By practicing mahamudra regularly, you will have a balanced breath in a very natural way.

Disciple: *What do you intend by moderation in food?*

Prajnananandaji: By food we intend all what we absorb: it can be through the eyes, ears, mouth or any sense organ. Food can be physical, mental and spiritual. Moderation in the intake of physical and mental food is very important.

MANTRAS

Disciple: *During first Kriya initiation you ask if we are using a mantra and if we are not, you give us one. Should we use this mantra during our meditation, and if so, at which point of our practice?*

Prajnananandaji: During first Kriya initiation we usually do not give instructions on the use of the mantra. In India, by tradition, the disciple receives a mantra during the initiation. During first Kriya initiation, if one does not have a mantra, we inscribe OM in both fontanel and on the tip of the tongue.

You can repeat the given mantra while concentrating in the 10 parts of the body.

Disciple: *Is one free to use other mantras and names of the Lord for japa-sadhana or should one only remain faithful to the given mantra?*

Prajnananandaji: The use of a mantra given by a teacher yields more results. A mantra given by the teacher is more powerful than any other mantra and at the same time it gives more results as it has more power than a mantra found in a book. When you are sick, you do not go and look for a medicine in a book, but you go to a doctor who will prescribe the correct medicine. With your doctor's prescription you will go to the pharmacy and you will buy the medicine. Usually, when you go to buy medicines without a prescription, the pharmacist answers that without the doctor's prescription he cannot give them to you. Similarly, a mantra received from a teacher yields the expected results. Mantras are not mere words, but words with a specific sound and they carry that specific and special energy transmitted by the teacher to the student.

NAMASMARANA, JAPA AND CHANTING

Disciple: *Some teach that the name is the boat to cross the river of samsara. Do you advise such a repetition of one of the names of the Lord and if so, does one have to continue for ever such a practice or is it only a first stage?*

Prajnananandaji: Gurudev used to say: 'If I go on repeating Hariharananda, Hariharananda, who will answer? I am Hariharananda. If I am Hariharananda then why am I calling and repeating Hariharananda? Who am I calling by repeating Hariharananda? I should repeat: "I AM THAT".

You are that power of God. You are that very name you are chanting. You are 'That' and you are to experience it. One has crossed the river of samsara when one experiences that the same name one remembers and goes on repeating is not at all different from "I AM THAT".

Gurudev often quoted; "Be always in tune with Divinity, that is the Supreme state."
We can therefore state that:

1) The meditative state is a lower stage than being always in tune with Divinity.

2) Chanting is a lower stage than the meditative state.

3) The lowest step is puja and worship.

To be established in the meditative state one should slowly go beyond the worship stage, then beyond the chanting stage or, anyhow, try and reach the point of chanting the name remembering its real meaning and experiencing it.

Disciple: *I was told that pranayama has effect only if accompanied by the repetition of one of God's names. Is Kriya breathing an exception?*

Prajnananandaji: In reality what we do during Kriya breathing is more effective than chanting the Lord's names only with the mouth as one is constantly aware of Divinity while focusing on light, vibration and sound. During Kriya breathing technique one is constantly aware of Divinity even if the mouth is not engaged in chanting God's names.

Disciple: *Is chanting only an extrovert state or does it help in achieving the introvert state?*

Prajnananandaji: Gurudev used to say that God has given man five sense organs and that, to discipline his life, man should only use his five sense organs to perceive God. With the mouth one should chant God's names, with the eyes one should only see sacred places but, to experience the transcendental reality, man has to go beyond the senses.

There is nothing wrong if beginners, when their mind is restless, chant God's names, but when their mind is calm and quiet, one should meditate.

Disciple: *Should kriyabans chant before meditating?*

Prajnananandaji: If you wish you can combine chanting and meditation. In spiritual life it is important to continuously remember God, so chanting is good, but it is more vital that one reaches the meditative state. There is a saying in our Vedic Scriptures: "Chant for a while, but it is far better to meditate and to be still. If restlessness is very strong, go on chanting a little more."

SOME ASPECTS OF HINDU CULTURE

Disciple: *Please give an explanation, for westerners' easier approach, of the most important names that represent the Lord, the Almighty in Hindu culture: Ishwara, Purusha, Mahapurusha, Brahman, Narayana, Purushottama, Siva, Brahma, Vishnu etcetera…..*

Prajnananandaji: So etcetera ….means "no end"!!!

Ishwara - Ishwara is the one who controls and regulates creation, as its Sanskrit root is ISH – ish dhatu means one who controls and regulates. So Ishwara is the controller and regulator of the world. When in English you exclaim: 'Oh Lord' the term Lord can be translated as Ishwara, but please do remember that Easwara is different from Brahman.

Purusha - The literal meaning in Sanskrit of the name Purusha is: one who is sleeping in the city. We can compare the city to creation, so Purusha, the formless power of God, is sleeping or hiding in the city. The body is the city, and the indwelling Sat, Purusha, is hiding in the body.Another meaning of Purusha is the masculine aspect of creation. The creator in the masculine form is Purusha and His feminine counterpart, the feminine aspect of creation, is Prakriti or Nature. Purusha with the help of Prakriti (Nature) makes creation go on.

Mahapurusha – Maha means great and Purusha means being. A great being, a super being. The name Mahapurusha is used for great souls, highly realized beings, noble souls. Mahapurusha means great Soul.

Narayana - Narayana is another name for Vishnu, the sustainer of the world. The name Narayana consists of two words joined together: Nara means the human being or living being and yana means the movement or activity. Narayana is the cause of all actions in a living being, Narayana is the cause of movement of breath. Narayana is the cause of the movements of the body. Narayana means the Soul in the body.

Brahman – The Sanskrit name Brahman can be translated in English as the Supreme or the greatest. Because of His greatness He is called Brahman. There is nothing beyond Brahman, nothing greater than Brahman. There is nothing beyond Brahman. Brahman is the soul in the body.

Purushottama - In Sanskrit the name Purushottama is composed by two words: Purusha and uttama. Uttama means superior or the best. Purusha means being, therefore it means the Supreme Being. In the 15th chapter of the Gita you can find full description of the qualities and meaning of Puroshottama.

Brahma – First in the Trinity, the Creator who created the universe with His cosmic mind. The creative power.

Vishnu – Second in the Trinity. Vishnu permeates and pervades the entire universe. The preservative power.

Siva – or Maheshvara – is the third in the Trinity. In Sanskrit the I in Siva bears a stroke on top. If one eliminates the letter 'I' from the name Siva, sva remains and sva means corps, a dead body. In this body there is a power that keeps it alive. This power is Siva, the sustaining power.

Disciple: *What is the meaning of the chakra that both Vishnu and Krishna hold in their hands?*

Prajnananandaji: A chakra is a disc. Krishna used it only twice: once to kill Sisupala and once when He ran towards Bhishma and Bhishma invited Him to use it. The symbolic meaning of the two Deities holding the chakra is Kala chakra, the wheel of time; the wheel of time is constantly rotating as time changes continuously. The wheel keeps on changing , but the one who holds it never changes. To go beyond time, kala, one has to worship mahakala, the Soul or God who is the supreme time beyond all measurements. Another meaning is movement symbolizing the progress we are to achieve in spiritual life. What is the inner meaning of Krishna killing Sisupala? Sisu means children and our thoughts are like our children. Sisupala was very restless and represents one who is always after pleasure and therefore many thoughts rise in his mind. These thoughts may be ego, hatred or jealousy type of thoughts. Therefore Krishna, by cutting Sisupala's head with the chakra teaches us we are to destroy our negative thoughts.

Disciple: *Why is Ganga worshipped?*

Prajnananandaji: In the Indian tradition Ganga is considered as the most sacred river and the greatest means of purification. People take a holy dip in Her waters to purify themselves. Shankara said that by taking even one drop of Ganga water one becomes immortal. What is the meaning? Just as there is a river Ganga outside, there is an inner Ganga, the Ganga of knowledge. Taking a bath in this jnana Ganga one becomes a jnani. Ganga is the life force and the body the universe. Ganga is known by three names:

1) The part that remains up in the domain of the devas or gods is called Suradhuni.

2) The Ganga that was brought down by the efforts of king Bhagiratha is called Bhagirathi.

3) When Ganga proceeds to the lower regions, to the patala, it is called Bhogavati.

The body is a miniature universe so, like the external Ganga, also the inner Ganga - prana shakti or life force - flows in three different rivers, three different flows. Every moment many emotions arise and they cause this inner Ganga to flow either downwards or upwards.

When Ganga, as prana shakti in our body flows downwards towards patalapuri – the materialistic and financial world – she becomes Bhogavati. Bhogas are the so called enjoyments that are located in the muladhara, svadhisthana and manipura chakras that are the centers for money, sex, food and drink.

When Ganga, as life force, stays in the middle part – the heart region – it causes various emotions. When the life force flows upward from the heart to sahasrara, this inner Ganga is also called devanadi. The nature of a person depends on where this life force is predominantly flowing. If one succeeds in keeping one's flow of life force upwards, eternal peace can be gained.

Disciple: *Please, further clarify the inner meaning about the Vedas' injunction to bathe in sacred rivers.*

Prajnananandaji: Rather than bathing in external holy rivers, what the Vedas extolled was: inner purification through bathing in the internal oasis of the Self. The eight tirthas (holy places) are: non-violence, truthfulness, forgiveness, compassion, knowledge, purity of the Self, straightforwardness, and liberation. All these eight virtues are in the neck centre.

When we dive into these eight holy rivers, as they are called, we will be free from the eight causes for human bondage: shame, hatred, fear, sorrow, jealousy, pride, ego and prejudice.

By bathing or filling ourselves with the eight divine qualities, we can purify our minds and escape the state of bondage.

Hindus believe that by taking a dip in holy rivers, like Ganga or Yamuna, they become pure. The body undoubtedly gets cleansed and because of the aspirant's strong belief, also the mind gets purified to a certain extent, but this is only temporary.

Disciple: *Baba, what is the essential message of Krishna's life?*

Prajnananandaji: Krishna's life is a constant example and lesson on how we should all be. His continuous attempts to resolve all crises with peaceful means, His willingness to forgive His enemies, His humility in being the messenger between two parties, the Pandavas and Kauravas, and finally His involvement in Arjuna's spiritual progress and how He encouraged him throughout his struggle towards enlightenment are all examples on how we should conduct our own lives.

Krishna's life, from the very beginning, was full of challenges. Lord Krishna had to face hostile threats and many attempts on His life from His very birth. He was born in a dark prison on a dark and gloomy night and from then onwards all His life thus becomes a metaphor of the soul's struggle to survive obstacles and dangers remaining pure, bright and whole. Throughout His childhood filled with dangers, despite poisoned milk, venomous snakes, an uncle who continuously attempted to kill Him and His displacement from a royal family to a peasant one, Krishna remained ever joyous, always content. Krishna, as a baby or a youth, as a friend or as a leader, stands out as the perfect example of how we should live each moment of our lives.

Disciple: *What does Avatar mean and what does one intend by full or partial Avatar?*

Prajnananandaji: The term Avatar means Incarnation of the Lord. Indian mythology gives a description of twenty four Avatars or Divine Incarnations manifesting Divinity either partially or fully. This means that the divine power is manifested either at a greater or lesser extent. We are all Avatars. The difference between them and us is that an Avatar knows the purpose for which He has come and we don't. So also Jesus was an Avatar and so was Moses and Mohammed. In our line of Masters Babaji was called Mahavatar, Great Avatar – Lahiri Mahasaya, was called Yogavatar – incarnation of Yoga, Shriyukteshwar was called Jnanavatar – incarnation of knowledge and Yogananda, Premavatar – incarnation of love. Krishna, in the *Bhagavad Gita* IV:7-8 explains to Arjuna the reason why the Lord incarnates again and again:

'Oh Arjuna! Whenever there is a rising trend of immorality, then I manifest Myself. In every age I manifest to give liberation to the good and to eliminate and destroy evil minded ones, to uphold morality, righteousness in the society.'

Meditate and you will realize we are all Avatars.

CREATION

Disciple: *Out of what did God create the universe?*

Prajnananandaji: God has created everything from Himself. The Mundaka Upanishad gives the example of the spider. The spider makes a cobweb out of his own saliva and then lives in this cobweb. The spider is the skillful creator and his saliva is the material cause. Out of this example you may understand that the entire creation is a transformation into energy. This energy, the material cause is God. God is both the creator and the instrumental cause as He has created everything out of His Own Self. Since creation was made from God alone, God is everywhere and therefore your own body is the temple of God. If you close your eyes and look within, God is there.

Disciple: *Which was the first element to be created and what was the order in which they were created?*

Prajnananandaji: Ether was the first. From ether came air, from air, fire and fire projected water and water the earth and plants were born, from plants came food and from food human beings arose.

THE MIND: THE ETERNAL MYSTERY

Disciple: *Is the mind a gift of God or just a handicap?*

Prajnananandaji: The mind is a special gift of God to human beings, we only have to train it so that it will become a useful tool for our spiritual development. The mind can keep us in bondage or it may become the door to evolution.

Disciple: *Then, kindly tell me why I still cannot sit with no thoughts?*

Prajnananandaji: Many thoughts make the mind very restless. A restless mind makes one very active and sometimes also hyperactive. In the beginning stages most minds are restless. Accept it and do not be too unhappy as, for beginners, it is almost a blessing till they have completely cleansed their mind from negative thoughts. The mind is a flow of thoughts, a chain of thoughts that never stop flowing. If you sit down with your eyes closed and you try to count your thoughts you will realize that, in only one minute, 20 thoughts have crossed your mind. To reach a concentrated state of mind you should reach the stage of having one single thought for a long period of time. Many thoughts, ideas, preferences, likes and dislikes and plans contradicting each other control your life.

When the mind is attached to the sense objects it is in bondage and, when it is free from the attachment, one is free. The mind alone is the cause of bondage and liberation, joy and pain. The mind can go outward towards the sense objects or inwards towards the source. Man has the capacity to channel and change the quality of his thoughts. By changing your thinking patterns you can change the quality of your life. You should train the mind not to be the cause of unhappiness, rather the cause of joy. You see the world according to your own mind: with a good mind you see only good and God's presence everywhere, but with a doubting mind everything becomes an object of doubt. So, it is only the mind that creates all the trouble, all the pain and unhappiness. Watch the mind and take care of it.

We can say that everyone has a political mind and a spiritual mind. With a political mind one looks through one's own inner equipment at the fault of others, always analyzing and criticizing others. With a political mind one always wants to change others. We all have this type of mind. Those who have a spiritual mind only try to change themselves. The spiritual-minded person constantly looks within trying to change and transform himself.

There are five different states of the mind:

1) confused
2) restless
3) scattered
4) concentrated
5) completely controlled.

The mind of a man always sleepy, idle and lacking discrimination is said to be in a confused state.

The mind of the majority of people is dynamic and restless. When it is restless the mind is full of desires and always looking for a change.

The mind absorbed in a particular pleasure for a longer period of time is said to be scattered: scattered in a particular sense pleasure (like overeating due to the taste pleasure).

A concentrated mind is a focused mind. The object of concentration can be either external or internal. A surgeon concentrates on an external object and a yogi concentrates inside. With a concentrated state of mind one can channel the mind towards the goal.

A completely controlled state of mind can be achieved through meditation and a God-conscious, balanced lifestyle. To reach this special state of mind one has to cleanse one's mind thoroughly till it is completely pure.

Disciple: *What is the purpose of the mind?*

Prajnananandaji: The mind is in between the body and the soul. The mind wants constant happiness, but does not know how to reach it. The mind wants love, but does not know where to find it. The purpose of the mind is to know who we are, but the mind itself, with its desires and restlessness is the main obstacle to perceive the soul. The mind goes on reminding us that we are the body and that we should enjoy this world making it difficult to allow us perceive the truth of the soul, that we are the soul and not the body. The goal of life, the purpose of the mind is to perceive and experience we are the soul.

Once the mind knows the goal, the game is over!

Through regular meditation, Kriya and conscious breathing one can achieve control over the mind. The shorter the breath, the calmer the mind. Be disciplined, analyze the mind, watch the mind and watch the breath. In reality the human mind is not happy with momentary gains and pleasures, it wants to dive deep and fly high to discover the treasures of the soul. If well trained the mind becomes your best ally. The mind is the cause of bondage but, at the same time, of liberation.

WAKEFUL, SLEEP, DREAM AND DEEP SLEEP STATES

Disciple: *Can there be happiness in this world? Where and what is happiness?"*

Prajnananandaji: Happiness is not outside, it is a state of calmness of the mind that one should constantly strive to preserve. Happiness is not to be found in good food, if food contained happiness, then by taking more food one would feel happier, but this is far from being true. Happiness is not in the sense objects or a nice holiday. Happiness is a state of mind that makes one see things in a positive way. The mind is restless when it goes outward but, during the deep sleep state, it is calm and quiet. During deep sleep the mind is at rest. The senses are not working and the breath is rhythmic. If one succeeds in keeping the senses under control and in breathing rhythmically one can attain a deep sleep-like state consciously. Meditation is a conscious effort to attain an even better state than deep sleep, a state that is beyond the waking, dream and deep sleep states called turiya. To reach this state one must, first of all attain a complete clean state of no thoughts and no mind. With concentration and rhythmic breathing we can attain such a state where one can enjoy more freedom and love.

Everyday we experience wakeful, dream and deep-sleep states. We have three planes of existence or bodies: one is the gross body, the second is the astral and the third body is the casual body. In the wakeful state, the body, mind and senses are all active. In the dream state the gross body is not active but the astral or subtle and casual bodies are active. Our subtle body is responsible for the dreams we experience. From the dream state we enter the deep-sleep state.

What happens during sleep? When you go to sleep your consciousness separates from your body, from your senses and your mind. At this point you are in a space where nothing exists any longer. In deep sleep you are in a blissful state. This bliss lasts as long as you are in that state of deep sleep. When you wake up you say: 'I slept so well, I was not aware of anything!' as in deep-sleep the world does not exist. In the wakeful state the mind plays in the world while in the dream state it plays with the world of our experiences. In deep-sleep the mind plays with ignorance.

Happiness is being in your natural state and free from all what is unnatural. Unhappiness and restlessness are unnatural. We should get rid of them in order to be constantly content and joyful.

Disciple: *In this so-called wakeful state everything appears to be real, so how can I say the world is only a projection of my mind?*

Prajnananandaji: Thirty years ago you were a student, a young bachelor starting his career with enthusiasm. You were not married and you had no children. Where was your wife and where were your children? Everything is in your mind only. In our daily life we have our own projections and also common projections. Have you ever tasted bitter gourd? Some people don't like bitter gourd as it is a very bitter vegetable. Personally I find it extremely good as I particularly enjoy bitter food. So, my projection is that bitter gourd is extremely good, while the common projection is that it s a very bitter vegetable. In this world there are many projections of likes and dislikes and they differ from person to person. Even if there are common projections, in a subtle way, the entire world is a projection of our own mind. If you go a little deeper you will understand.

GUNAS

Disciple: *How do the gunas affect us?*

Prajnananandaji: Human nature and behaviour are the result of the three fold qualities of nature or gunas that are present within each one of us. Every person has a mixture of these three qualities with one of them predominating. People can be divided into groups depending on the predominant quality of their mind. The three gunas are: Sattva, Rajas, Tamas.

Sattva is purity, rajas is activity and tamas is inertia. When a person is sattvic he is contemplative, mature and gives priority to human values and the real goal of life. When a person is mostly rajasic he is still attracted by making money, a nice home or a big car and he is very active and ambitious. When a person is tamasic he is often dull, lazy and still attracted by animal tendencies.

In ancient times the Indian caste system depended on the predominant quality and the activity of a person so each human being becomes a brahmin, a ksatriya, a vaisya or a sudra depending on his predominant quality and on the nature of the work he is doing at a particular time. When a person is engaged in taking care of body, he becomes a sudra: when engaged in making money, he becomes a vaisya, when he is exercising his body to maintain it in good health, he becomes a ksatriya and when he tries to meditate, read the sacred Scriptures or is intent in any religious or spiritual activity, at that time he becomes a brahmana.

Disciple: *Should one balance the three qualities or go beyond?*

Prajnananandaji: First one should balance them and later on go beyond.

DESTINY AND FREE WILL

Disciple: *Destiny, karma and free will confuse me. Please clear my* comprehension. *If God is omnipresent and omniscient He knows our past but also our future, so our actions are already fixed. Where is our free will if God knows everything?.*

Prajnananandaji: First of all, eliminate all your buts and ifs from your mind. This creation is a play, a divine play. From your individual viewpoint thinking of God's Omniscience is stupidity. We are all divine actors in this divine drama. Apart from the divine, cosmic drama, there is our own individual drama. It is a dream inside the dream. There is a cosmic dream and in the cosmic dream we are the dream objects of God. We dream inside the dream. It may sound funny, but this is how it is. The divine play is going on in a cosmic way and we enact our own individual play due to our ego forgetting God and the goal of life. When we forget God in our individual play, we bring more ego in our life. We think we are the doers, our ego is the obstacle to happiness, it is the primary cause of many of our sufferings. We are God's children, but as we have been ignoring this basic truth through many lives, we still feel we are separate from God. This is only apparent. Notwithstanding having ignored God, we have all the possibilities to overcome all our mistakes here and now.

As one has to bear the results of one's past egoist actions, one's present karma is mainly due to one's own choices. You have some freedom, but not complete freedom. We are not slaves of destiny, but responsible for our own actual situation as we ourselves through our own actions, have created our own destiny. With effort, meditation and prayer one can counteract the effects of one's actions, so destiny can be modified.

Many people ask me if there exists individual freedom or if we are guided by our own karma. The words I can use are fate, destiny and luck. Up to my 20s I had been a serious asthma patient and suffered continuously. What I brought into this life was individual destiny. I followed the strict discipline of Kriya Yoga and this spiritual endevour helped me and now I am absolutely well. So one has the free will to make things better through spiritual practices. We can compare the freewill God has given us to the length of the rope that the cowherds allow a cow when tying it to a tree.

MANAS, BUDDHI, AHAMKARA

Disciple; *What is the relationship between manas, buddhi and ahamkara?*

Prajnananandaji: To explain this we have to use an example. Suppose you have a car, if the car breaks down you have some tools to fix it, don't you? Similarly, this body is like a car, the soul is the driver and in the body there are some tools. They are called inner and outer instruments.

The inner instruments are four and they are called anthakarana: mind, buddhi, citta and ego.

1) The mind is the doubting and confusing faculty, the mind deliberates but it cannot decide.

2) The intellect is the deciding and discriminating faculty. When you have some doubts, the intellect will take the decision as it has a quality of rationality and it allows a person to think. This determining and decision making capacity improves when one meditates more.

3) The ego is the doer-ship faculty. When one is intoxicated by ego, he mistakenly believes himself to be the central cause of all events that take place around him, forgetting all is God.

4) Citta is the memory that allows us to remember, but also the faculty of inquiry. This Sanskrit word citta is usually translated as mind stuff.

These four constitute the major part of the astral body or subtle body. As the body grows the mind, citta, buddhi and ahamkara also grow, the type of equipment we have depends on the environment one is born into.

The soul is the driver or the mechanic who knows how to use the tools in a proper way. These four tools are useful only if you know how to use them, but if you do not, you are in trouble. All is fine if you know how to use the ego and the mind. They are the instruments and the soul is the driver who knows how to use them and how to repair them.

Disciple: *Which was manifested first in creation? Citta, buddhi, ahamkara or manas?*

Prajnananandaji: At the beginning of creation consciousness was first manifested in the form of citta, in the form of thought. When thought became gross, ego developed, when ego grew and that sense of I ness became gross, buddhi developed, when the intellect became gross, the mind developed.

DHARMA

Disciple: *The term dharma is often confusing, will you give me the exact meaning?*

Prajnananandaji: The Sanskrit term dharma is very difficult to translate into English and it has various different meanings. The ordinary meaning is religion, as in Hindu Dharma, but dharma has a much wider spectrum of meanings.

One of the meanings is the inherent nature of a substance: the nature of water is to be cool and to flow downwards. When it does not flow, under zero degrees, it becomes ice.

Another meaning is duty and responsibility in society. We play different roles as wife or husband, as children, as mother or father, as student or teacher. Whatever you may be, you have specific duties and responsibilities to fulfill.

SATSANG

Disciple: *What is satsang?*

Prajnananandaji: Let us start by clarifying that the injunction 'avoid bad company' does not only mean you have to avoid a bad person that is pulling you down and tempting you with superficial worldly issues, but it can also be the wrong type of music, bad movies, bad programs on television and bad books. Anything that makes you weak and brings down your moral and ethical values is bad company.

On the contrary, saints, good books, a good program on TV, etc are all good company. So what is satsang? Satsang is generally understood as being in the company of the saints and enlightened ones, but in truth it means to be in the company of one's soul.

PLAY OF MAYA

Disciple: *How does the splendour of the Atma affect the mind, the senses, and the body?*

Prajnananandaji: Without the soul they are inert. Because of the presence of the soul they become active: without soul they are useless, inert, dead.

Disciple: *Where does the ' I ' consciousness come from?*

Prajnananandaji: If this 'I' consciousness is equal to God consciousness in an absolute sense, then it comes from your practice; if this I refers to the ego, then it comes from ignorance.

Disciple: *Is there really an outside and an inside? Worldly and spiritual? Good and bad?*

Prajnananandaji: In reality no, but in the world of existence yes. They are all relative and exist only from an individual point of view.

Disciple: *Up to which point are we to talk about jivatma and Paramatma, if they are ONE?*

Prajnananandaji: Once you experience and realize, there is no difference. But as long as you do not realize it, there is duality.

Disciple: *What is meant by grace of God?*

Prajnananandaji: Your effort comes first and God's grace comes next. When we take a few steps towards Him He will take a hundred steps to help us. One can consider Grace as the money one has deposited in a bank account through previous actions. One can draw on such a deposit any check and also, when balance is nil ask for a loan, but sooner or later one will have to return the grace received on loan. Grace is always there, you must turn your pot upwards with sadhana to be able to receive it.

Disciple: *As only God exists, what limits us still and makes us talk about jivatma?*

Prajnananandaji: It is the ego and ignorance.

Disciple: *Will there always be this confusion till all body consciousness and the complete sense of I and mine has disappeared?*

Prajnananandaji: Yes.

REBIRTH

Disciple: *Is there really rebirth and why?*

Prajnananandaji: If there were no rebirth it would be very difficult for you to understand many things in life.

I will quote from *Mundaka Upanishad* III.ii.2:

'The man with desires and who keeps brooding on them has repeated rebirths. When the goal is attained and man perfected, desires will all completely vanish by themselves.'

FOOD HABITS

Disciple: *Could you kindly also give us some directions on food habits as I have heard so many different opinions that I now am quite confused.*

Prajnananandaji: Healthy eating habits will raise our body energy and give the needed drive to accomplish our daily routine. A nourishing breakfast is essential. Fresh fruits and vegetables are an integral part of a healthy diet. We should choose our food taking in consideration a balanced intake of proteins, carbohydrates, fat, vitamins and minerals. It is important to include plenty of vegetables as fiber and fruit are very important in one's diet. We should choose food that is palatable and healthy. Not too spicy, not too hot, not salty. Our needs are much, much less than our greed!! Be moderate and chose a simple diet. By simple what do I mean? If to absorb carbohydrates I choose to eat some potatoes, I have the choice to prepare them either as curry, fried chips or just as plain boiled potatoes. Boiled potatoes is the simplest way of cooking, so choose the simplest and most natural way. Am I clear?

Try to choose natural food and try to become less dependent on packaged foods that have added chemicals and unknown ingredients. Eat moderately, three times a day and, as a principle, avoid in-between snacks and never indulge in food.

Yogis keep their tongue rolled up and this also means that they keep their tongue under control. By keeping their tongue under control, they keep their life under control. As by keeping their tongue rolled up it affects not only what they eat, but also what they say, their life is filled with peace and calmness.

When one leaves the dining room, the stomach should only be half full. Half full of food and the other half full of water.

Water is a very important. To avoid constipation, drink plenty of water. Daily correct intake of water is very important and beneficial also to the skin. It cleanses the skin and purifies the internal organs. A healthy way to lose weight is to drink a glass of water before eating as this will fill up the stomach and, consequently, the food intake will be reduced. One can sip some water while eating, but it is absolutely unhealthy to drink after one has finished eating. Refrain from drinking any type of liquid for thirty or forty minutes.

To maintain a state of calmness and aid digestion one should chew the food very slowly and thoroughly. Gurudev used to say one had to chew a hundred times before swallowing the food.

In the evenings one should eat lightly and at least three hours before going to bed. A heavy stomach disturbs our sleep.

One should always pray before eating. Never start eating without having, first, offered your food to God and, from time to time, observe some fasting as it will increase one's will power.

HUMAN VALUES

Disciple: *Which are the most important human values we should enhance to reach the goal of life?*

Prajnananandaji: To be successful we need to cultivate a lifestyle enriched with values. Just as a flower should not only be beautiful, but it should also spread a wonderful fragrance, we should incorporate eternal values in our daily life.

The most important human values are: truthfulness, honesty, simplicity, fearlessness and devotion.

SURRENDER

Disciple: *What is the idea of surrender? What do we have to surrender?*

Prajnananandaji: What do you have to do to overcome the waves of the ocean? You either jump the waves or you bend your head down and you dive in, don't you? Also in life we have to bend our head a little and surrender to God just as you surrender to the ocean. We do have control over many circumstances, but not over all that happens in our lives. Who is in control when we realize we are helpless? When we are not totally in control, God's cosmic plan and our past karma, mixed together, are in control. To surrender means to love God. Understanding the omnipresence of God is surrender. Meditation is a way of surrendering to God. When circumstances are critical, you do your best, but if your efforts are useless, all you should do is to surrender to His will with faith and trust. When a child depends completely on his mother, he is safe. Think of God as your mother and of yourself as the child and the love you feel will give enough strength to overcome any problem. There are two ways: either you take up the attitude of the kitten that allows its mother to move it here and there in case of danger or the attitude of the baby monkey who clings to its mother and never lets go. To surrender means trusting God to take care of you. In any circumstance love God.

Disciple: *What is this drama of human life all about?*

Prajnananandaji: Once you have accepted life as a drama, accept it. If the dream is realized as such, then the world is done with. God's creation is a drama for entertainment. In the drama of human life sometimes you experience pleasure and sometimes pain. Life is for progress and evolution and one should listen to the promptings of God with rapt attention in order not to get into problems.

KARMA

Disciple: *What does prarabdha karma and samskara mean?*

Prajnananandaji: Past lives influence this present lifetime and this present life influences the future. So be careful today and spend every moment in God consciousness. Yesterday you were in your own home. You spent the night traveling to be here at the retreat. Now you are here enjoying our talk. The result of all your efforts brought you here. Prarabdha is the accumulated effect of past karma or actions. Today you are enjoying the fruit of your past actions. Would you have been allowed here at the retreat if you had not taken initiation some years ago?

The word samskara means tendency or habit. Once formed, a habit becomes powerful, so powerful that it is difficult to overcome. If one repeatedly draws a line on a stone with some iron nails, a groove will form that cannot be erased. To change a habit one has to change one's outlook. Realize that no external object can give you happiness and peace of mind, but only temporary and limited happiness. Once this temporary happiness vanishes one is again unhappy. To attain eternal happiness one has to go inside.

SOUL

Disciple: *Baba, kindly give us a definition of the soul!*

Prajnananandaji: In the Bible the soul is described as the image of God. The soul is immortal and ever pure. Without the soul, the body and the senses are inert. Without the power of the soul a body is as useless as a bulb when there is no electricity.

The soul appears to be covered by the body and inner instruments. If the covering is clean the light of the soul shines bright. If the covering is dirty, the light is obstructed. Our own body and mind cover the soul. The mind is in-between the body and the soul, thus preventing us from perceiving the soul. If the mind is transparent, one can perceive the soul. Take the example of a mala or rosary: the thread represents the soul and the beads are our thoughts. If the beads are transparent the thread can be seen in its splendorous fullness.

The soul is the supreme source of energy in the body. You can compare it to the main electrical switch, which controls all the lights in the house supplying energy to the various outlets. The soul is the main source of energy for the eyes to see, the ears to hear, the nose to smell, the skin to feel and the mouth to taste. The soul is connected with the Supreme Source, God, just as the main electrical switch is connected to a power house or power generator and can never be disconnected.

The soul is ever free and never in bondage. It lives in a body for a while, when the soul abandons the body, there is no life. The brain, all the body parts and senses function thanks to the soul energy. Also the mind can think only as long as the soul is in the body. The

Upanishadic Scriptures declare that the soul is Sat Chit Ananda – existence, awareness and bliss. The soul is immortal, eternal knowledge and pure bliss. The soul is ever free and never in bondage.

Om Tat Sat Om

GLOSSARY

abhyasa	practice.
acharya	preceptor, spiritual guide, one who points the way to the spiritual path.
ahankaara	ego, doership, vanity and pride
ahimsa	non-violence, non-injury, maintaining love for all.
ananda	divine bliss, supreme joy.
Anandamoyee Ma	a prominent female saint of India of the 20th century.
Ananta	eldest brother of Mukunda (Yogananda).
anthakarana	inner instrument, consisting of mind, intellect, ego and memory.
antra	inner.
asana	seat; sitting posture, a place to sit for prayer and meditation.
ashrama	hermitage; four stages of life accepted by the old traditional Indian civilization: celibacy, household, retirement to the forest and renunciation.
Ashutosh Mukhopadhyaya	
	also known as Shastri Mahasaya, later Hamsa Swami Kevalananda.
atma or atman	"the Self", the soul.
atma jnana	self-knowledge.
atma karma	actions leading to self-knowledge.

atma ram	one who obtains inner peace, bliss and joy while being engrossed in soul-consciousness.
Balananda Brahmachari	disciple of Lahiri Mahasaya.
Basukumar Bagchi	premonastic name of Swami Dhirananda, childhood friend of Mukunda (Yogananda) and Manmohan (Swami Satyananda).
Bhagavad Gita	a sacred text of eighteen chapters; a dialogue between Shri Krishna and Arjuna at the start of the battle of the *Mahabharata*.
Bhagavati Charan Ghosh	father of Mukunda (Yogananda).
bhakta	devotee, disciple, worshipper, one who follows the path of devotion
bhakti	devotion, divine love.
bhandara	congregation of monks, which ends with a sumptuous feast.
bhramari mudra	a state of hearing nothing during meditation.
braahmana	one of the four principal castes, the priestly caste
Brahma	soul, *Krishna*; God in His aspect as creator; one aspect of the Vedic trinity.
brahma-granthi	creative knot, its location is in the lower three chakras in the body.
brahmachari	celibate *sadhaka*, one who disciplines the lower mind, one who roams in God-consciousness.
Brahmachari Keshavananda	a disciple of Lahiri Mahasaya.
brahmacharya	literally means celibacy and sense-control; esoterically it means "to roam in God", i.e. to live in constant God-consciousness.

Brahman	God the formless, the Absolute.
brahmanda	the complete notion of the Universe.
Brahmasutra	one of the three fundamental scriptures (known collectively as *prasthana trayi*) for God-realization, written by *Maharshi Vyasa*.
brahmin	the first caste in the ancient Vedic social system of priests and teachers; metaphorically those who are on the spiritual path; to be in God (*brahman*).
buddhi	intellect, the faculty of decision making in the body.
chaitanya	awareness, consciousness.
chakra	the energy centers in the body described by the yogis, located inside the spine and brain.
chaturmaasi	four lunar months of monsoon starting from July full moon considered as holy by the monks of India for study and contemplation
chidabhas	reflective consciousness.
citta	the memory aspect of the mind, recollection, investigating aspect; from the root *cit* – consciousness.
chorakothari	a Bengali word for the place in the house where people kept their treasure in the old times.
darshan	communion with the Lord; blessing of a realized soul; holy vision or experience; path of knowledge; philosophy.

dervesha	Muslim mystic.
dharma	morality, duty, religion, responsibility, nature, quality and above all a way of life.
dhoti	Indian handloom cloth for men.
dhyana	meditation, reflection, contemplation.
Durga Puja	the celebration of the worship of the Divine Mother in the fall (September/October) as well as in the spring (March/April).
fakir	Muslim monk.
gayatri mantra	the 24-syllable Vedic mantra for spiritual evolution and liberation.
grihastha	householder.
guru	preceptor, Master, the realized one.
gurukulam	Ashram where the guru and his disciples lived together
Gurudeva	respected Master.
guru kripa	guru's grace.
Gyana Prabha Ghosh	mother of Mukunda (Yogananda).
ham	the gross body or instrument of the soul. The soul is the doer and the gross body is the instrument. It can also refer to the ego and to exhalation of breath.
Hamsa Swami Kevalananda	also known as Shastri Mahasaya (Ashutosh), a disciple of Lahiri Mahasaya and a great Sanskrit scholar.
Hamsa Swami	a swami who is advanced in meditation.

Haripada Bhattacharjee	father of Rabinarayan (Paramahamsa Hariharananda).
Ikshwaku	a king of the Solar Dynasty.
ishwara	the lord, an epithet of Shiva, the ruler
ishwara pranidhana	to live in God or to offer everything to God.
japa	the chanting, repeated chanting of mantra
Jagadguru Shrimat Swami Bharati Krishna Teerthajee	Shankaracharya of Puri who initiated Paramahamsa Hariharananda into *sannyasa*.
jivatamaa	individual self
Jnana Yoga	the path of reasoning and discrimination; yoga of knowledge.
jnana	knowledge of the essence and hidden meaning of all the holy books.
jnaani	a person with knowledge
Kabir	a saint, mystic poet of the 15th century, devotee of Ramananda, who inspired both Hindus and Muslims to meditate and follow the spiritual path.
Kadambini Devi	mother of Priyanath (Shriyukteshwar).
kalaa	quality, the growth of moon after the new moon
Kaala	time, time spirit, an epithet of Shiva
Kali Dasi Devi	wife of Shri Sanyal Mahasaya.
kamini	women.
kanchana	wealth, gold.
karma	action, duty; the law of cause and effect.

karmakanda	various rituals of the *Vedas*.
Karma Yoga	union with God through action, yoga of action.
Kashimani Devi	wife of Lahiri Mahasaya.
khechari mudra	a special *mudra* practiced in yoga. It is derived from *kha* ("space") and *char* ("to roam") - to roam in the formless stage of meditation.
kri	any work, activity or action.
Krishna	the divine incarnation of Vishnu; teacher of the *Bhagavad Gita*; made of *krishi*, "cultivation" (of the body land), and *na*, the power of God. Lord Krishna represents the indwelling Self who is conductor of the body.
kriya	action with consciousness of Self.
Kriya Yoga	the science of self-control and self-realization through meditation.
kriyavan	one who practices Kriya Yoga.
ksatriya	the warrior class
Kshetranath	father of Priyanath (Shriyukteshwar).
Kumbha Mela	a spiritual congregation of monks, saints and spiritual teachers held in four different holy cities of India during three-year intervals.
kutastha	"anvil", changeless; metaphorically, designates the soul center, the unchanging 'anvil' on which the different life-experiences are molded.

lila, leela	divine play.
Lord Jagannath	the Lord of the Universe, the presiding deity in the holy city of Puri, in the state of Orissa.
maanas	mental, silently
maayaa	illusive power
Mahabharata	the great Indian epic containing the *Bhagavad Gita*.
mahaakaala	an epithet of Shiva
Mahamaya	great delusive power; also a name of the Divine Mother.
mahamuni	great saint.
mahaamudra	a yogic exercise, literally a great treasure
mahaapurusha	a great soul, a saint or holy man
Maharshi Vyasa	the Master of masters, the great sage who composed and compiled the epic *Mahabharata*, *Brahmasutras* and other scriptures.
mahasamadhi	final and conscious exit of the earthly body by a realized yogi.
Mahatma Gandhi	humanist, propounder of peace and non-violence, spiritual leader and freedom fighter in India.
manasic	of the mind.
Manmohan Mazumdar	premonastic name of Swami Satyananda.
Manu	considered as the father of mankind in India, the Noah of Indian mythology; author of a book designing a moral way of life.

Master Mahasaya	Mahendranath Gupta, a scholar and educator, disciple of Shri Ramakrishna, author of: "*Gospel of Ramakrishna*".
Matital Thakur	first disciple of Shriyukteshwar.
moha	delusion, dejection, and infatuation.
Mohini Mohan Mazumdar	father of Manmohan (Swami Satyananda).
mudra	a yogic technique or posture for controlling life force or for ritual purposes.
Mukunda	premonastic name of Yogananda.
naamasmarana	mental remembrance of Lord's name
naraayana	an epithet of Vishnu the second of the Hindu Trinity.
Nabinkali Devi	mother of Rabinarayan (Paramahamsa Hariharananda).
Nanga Baba Digambara Paramahamsa	a naked realized monk who lived in Puri.
nirvaana	liberation, freedom and a state of no breath.
nirvikalpa samadhi	state of no pulse and no breath, of total cessation of all activities of the body, mind, thought, intellect and ego; complete absorption in God-consciousness.
Panchanan Bhattacharya	the foremost householder disciple of Lahiri Mahasaya, published many yogic interpretations of the scriptures.
Paramahamsa Pranavananda	a disciple of Lahiri Mahasaya.
Paramahamsa	"supreme swan" (the swan is the only creature that is capable of separating the essence of the milk from water); the

liberated soul; an ascetic of the highest order; a realized Master who, having attained the supreme yogic state of *nirvikalpa samadhi*, can always distinguish the real (*sa*) from the unreal (*ham*).

paramatma	Supreme Self, God
paravastha	super-conscious state, the state of extreme tranquility.
parivrajaka	wandering monk.
prajna	wisdom.
prana	"life", life-force or breath; one of the five main *pranas* (vital energies), responsible for absorption; metaphysically, *prana* refers to exhalation.
pranayma	technique of regulating breath.
prarabdha	the accumulated effect of past *karma* or past actions giving fruit in this life.
priya	loving.
Priyanath	premonastic name of Shriyukteshwar.
punjabi	a native attire of India.
purusha	indwelling self, person
purushothama	the cosmic person, the Lord
praana	the vital energy, life force, the breath
Rabinarayan	*brahmachari* name of Paramahamsa Hariharananda.
Rabindranath	premonastic name of Paramahamsa Hariharananda.

Rabindranath Tagore	famous Bengali poet and Nobel laureate, the first Asian to get such honour for his poems 'Geetanjali'.
Rajarshi Janaka	a great king who reached self-realization.
rajasic	active, restless.
Rama	God-incarnate, disciple of *Vasistha*, he is considered an incarnation of *Vishnu*.
Ramana Maharshi	a realized soul, a saint who lived in the holy hill of Arunachal, South India.
rishi	"seer", man of right vision and action, also known as a sage.
rudra-granthi	the destructive or dissolutive energy located in the upper part of spine and lower brain, vishuddha and ajna chakra.
sa	the real doer, the soul; it can also refer to inhalation of breath.
sadhaka	"practitioner", aspirant, spiritual seeker.
sadhana	"means of attaining realization", sincere spiritual endeavour.
sadhusanga	company of holy men.
samadhi	merged and engrossed in God-consciousness; realization.
samskaras	impressions of previous thoughts and actions; latent tendencies.
sannyasi	a swami, a renunciate monk.
satguru	divine Master; title attributed to a loving, spiritual preceptor.
satsang	good company, fellowship with the self

satsanga	"good company, spiritual communion"; to be established in the Self.
sattva	purity, one of the triple qualities of nature, calmness
satya	truth.
seva	selfless service.
shambhavi mudra	a yogic practice of meditation with the eyes open to perceive the divine light.
Shankara	a great 6th century spiritual Master, incarnation of Lord *Shiva*, who revived the monastic tradition in India.
shanti	serenity, peace.
Shastri Mahasaya	later known as Hamsa Swami Kevalananda.
Shiva	the destructive aspect of God; one aspect of the Vedic trinity.
shraddha	deep desire for spirituality, faith or love.
shri	a name of goddess Lakshmi; as a prefix, a title of respect, like the English "Sir".
Shri Bijay Krishna Chattopadhyaya	a householder and a renowned realized Master, first guru of Paramahamsa Hariharananda.
Shri Chaitanya Mahaprabhu	also known as Shri Gouranga, a divine Master and great mystic saint of the 15th century, promoter of the *bhakti* movement.
Shri Krittibash Ojha	author and translator of many Holy Scriptures in Bengali including the *Mahabharata*.

Shri Ramakrishna Paramahamsa
a great 19th century saint and guru of Swami *Vivekananda*.

Shri Shyama Charan   another name of Shri Lahiri Mahasaya.

Shri Sitarama Das Omkarnath
a renowned *vaishnava* saint; guided thousands of disciples to the path of spirituality, also a *kriyavan*, initiated by Ram Gopal Majumdar, and a cousin of our beloved Gurudev Paramahamsa Hariharananda.

shudra   the fourth caste of the Hindus

siddhi   accomplishment, perfection, namely, attaining the state of *nirvikalpa samadhi*, becoming merged in God-consciousness.

smrutisastras   scriptures of ethics and morality.

sthita prajna   "established in wisdom", one who feels that whatever he sees, thinks, or experiences is the power of God.

sushumna   energy channel in the center of the spine.

svadhyaya   study of scriptures; comes from *sva* (soul) plus *adhyaya* (culture or study); to study one's own Self is soul culture.

swami   Master, a spiritual preceptor; one who has renounced worldly activities in order to dedicate his life to God.

Swami Dhirananda   Basukumar Bagchi, childhood friend of Mukunda (Yogananda).

Swami Jnanananda   head of the Bharat Dharma Mahamanda monastery, a man of great wisdom who

encouraged the initiation of Priyanath into
monkhood.

Swami Krishnadayal Giri the guru by whom Shriyukteshwar was
initiated into monkhood.

Swami Vishuddhananda Paramahamsa
also known as the "perfume saint", a highly
evolved soul.

Swami Vivekananda disciple of Shri *Ramakrishna* and a
contemporary of Shriyukteshwar; first to
bring vedantic philosophy to the West.

tamas the quality of inertia, laziness

tapas ordinarily this means doing penance and
austerities, but the metaphorical meaning
is to watch the breath as an oblation into
holy fire that maintains the body's heat.

Tapas means that in every breath one loves God
and remains alert.

Taravasini Devi mother of Manmohan (Swami Satyananda).

tattva element, principles, inner meaning.

turiya the fourth state, the state of realization

tyaga abandonment; it refers to renunciation of
all action, but not outwardly. Inner
detachment is possible only when one is
meditating sincerely and surrendering
completely to the will of God.

upanayana sacred thread ceremony.

Upanishad last part of the *Vedas*, also known as
vedanta.

vairagya detachment, state of dispassion.

Glossary

vaishnava	worshipper of *Vishnu*.
vaishya	the business class
vanaprastha	life of non-attachment and service, third stage of life; retiring to the forest.
Vasishtha	a sage, guru of *Rama*.
Vedanta	"the end or last portion (*anta*) of the *Vedas*"; another name for the *Upanishads*; state of total knowledge.
Vedas	the most ancient recorded scriptures of self- knowledge.
vichara	analysis, interpretation, discussion.
Vishnu	the preserving or sustaining aspect of God; one aspect of the Vedic trinity.
vishnu -granthi	the knot of sustenance located in the heart center, anahata chakra
Vivasvan	the first king of the Solar Dynasty.
ya	the power of the soul.
yoga	one of the six main branches of Indian philosophy, popularized by Sage Patanjali. It is also a way of life, which allows one to achieve union with the supreme Self while one is keeping body, mind and spirit fit through its practice.
yogacharya	a spiritual teacher of yoga.
yogi	one who practices yoga, one who is constantly united with the supreme Self.

BIRTHDAYS AND COMMEMORATIONS

Birthday of Lahiri Mahasaya	30th of Sept. 1828
Mahasamadhi of Lahiri Mahasaya	26th of Sept. 1895
Birthday of Shriyukteshwar	10th of May 1855
Mahasamadhi of Shriyukteshwar	9th of March 1936
Birthday of Bhupendranath Sanyal	20th of Jan. 1877
Mahasamadhi of Bhupendranath Sanyal	18th of Jan. 1962
Birthday of Paramahamsa Yogananda	5th of Jan. 1893
Mahasamadhi of Paramahamsa Yogananda	7th of March 1952
Birthday of Swami Satyananda	17th of Nov. 1896
Mahasamadhi of Swami Satyananda	2nd of Aug. 1971
Birthday of Paramahamsa Hariharananda	27th of May 1907
Mahasamadhi of Paramahamsa Hariharananda	3rd of Dec. 2002
Birthday of Paramahamsa Prajnanananda	10th of Aug 1960

Paramahamsa Prajnanananda is the current spiritual leader of the Kriya Yoga international organization. This organization was founded by his master, Paramahamsa Hariharananda, who spread the teachings of Kriya Yoga all over the world. Paramahamsa Hariharananda was Swami Shriyukteshwar and Paramahamsa Yogananda's most outstanding direct disciple, one of the greatest realized Kriya Yoga masters in the lineage of Mahavatar Babaji Maharaj and Lahiri Mahasaya.

Born in Orissa, Paramahamsa Prajnanananda was raised in a profound spiritual environment that inspired his search for Truth. He received his higher education in Cuttack and became a professor of economics there. In 1980, while still a student, he met Paramahamsa Hariharananda, who initiated him into Kriya Yoga, then fifteen years later, into the sacred path of *sannyas*. After only three years, at the early age of 39, his master conferred upon him the highest title of Paramahamsa, a designation reserved for monks and saints who have attained the summit of realization.

Enriched by his own direct experience, fathomless wisdom, and deep love for humanity, Paramahamsa Prajnanananda guides and inspires spiritual seekers, a living example of how to fulfill one's infinite potential. In addition to running the main ashrams in Puri, Cuttack, Vienna, and Miami, Prajnananandaji spreads spiritual knowledge and the ancient science of Kriya Yoga by holding seminars and retreats all over the world. Prajnana Mission, founded by Paramahamsa Prajnanananda, provides service to humanity with free medical assistance units and centers, residential schools for the poor, and many other charitable and educational activities.

Author of many books on the science of yoga, practical guidelines to the application of the wisdom of Vedantic philosophy, and insightful metaphorical commentaries on the major holy scriptures and world religions, Paramahamsa Prajnanananda binds and bridges Eastern and Western cultures with a harmonious, fresh, and non-sectarian approach.

KRIYA YOGA

The ancient history of Kriya Yoga is mystifying and mesmerizing. Its mysterious origins are an intermingling of mythology, history, and science that date from the dawn of human consciousness. Saints and sages of India have long practiced and spread the science of yoga. Kriya Yoga is a very ancient and effective yogic science as well as an age-old tradition that has been practiced by seers, saints, and sages since time immemorial.

In Indian mythology, even Rama and Krishna practiced and taught the Kriya meditation technique. Kriya practices were explained by the rishis in the Upanishads, by Sage Vasishtha in Yoga Vasishtha, and by Maharshi Patañjali in his Yoga Sutra.

The Bhagavad Gita (4:1) says that God first revealed the Kriya technique to Vivashvan, then Vivashvan passed it to his son Manu, the seventh of the fourteen Manus or progenitors of the human race. Manu then transmitted it to his son Ikshvaku, founder of the first dynasty of kings in ancient India. From then on this technique was transmitted from father to son, which metaphorically means from master to disciple, through direct oral transmission. Apparently lost in the increasing spiritual decline of later epochs, these teachings were revived by the timeless Mahavatar Babaji Maharaj in 1861, who named the technique "Kriya Yoga."

KRIYA YOGA CONTACTS

Kriya Yoga Centre Vienna
Pottendorferstrasse 69 A-2523 Tattendorf Austria
Tel: 0043 2253 81491   Fax: 0043 2253 80462
E-mail: kriya.yoga.centre@aon.at Web:www.kriyayoga-europe.org

Hariharananda Gurukulam
P.O. Chaitana, Balighai, Puri 750002, Orissa, India
Tel/Fax: 0091 6752 246644 Tel/Fax: 0091 6752 246788
E-mail: pmission@sify.com Web: www.prajnanamission.org

KRIYA YOGA CONTACTS

Kriya Yoga Institute
P.O. Box 924615 Homestead, FL 33092-4615 USA
Tel: 001 305 2471960 Fax: 001 305 2481951
E-mail: institute@ kriya.org Web: www.kriya.org

Kriya Yoga Center
Heezerweg 7, Sterksel, NL-6029 PP, Holland
Tel: 0031 40 2265576 Fax: 0031 40 2265612
E-mail: kriya.yoga@worldonline.nl

Available Books On Yoga, Philosophy And Spirituality

by Swami Satyananda Giri

Yogananda Sanga, ISBN 3-902038-22-5

by Paramahamsa Hariharananda

Kriya Yoga: The Scientific Process of Soul Culture and the Essence of all Religions, ISBN 81-86713-05-0

Each Human Body is a Bhagavad Gita, ISBN 81-87825-06-5

Bhagavad Gita in the Light of Kriya Yoga, Volume I: ISBN 0-9639107-0-1, Volume II: ISBN 0-9639107-1-X, Volume III: ISBN 0-9639107-2-8

Isha Upanishad, ISBN 85-081923

by Paramahamsa Prajnanananda

Mahavatar Babaji: The Eternal Light of God, ISBN 3-902038-28-4

Lahiri Mahasaya: Fountainhead of Kriya Yoga, ISBN 3-901665-22-6

Swami Shriyukteshwar: Incarnation of Wisdom, ISBN 3-901665-23-4

The Lineage of Kriya Yoga Masters, ISBN 3-902038-13-6

My Time with the Master, ISBN 3-902038-08-X

Discourses on the Bhagavad Gita, Volume I, ISBN 3-901665-25-0, Volume II, ISBN 3-901665-26-9

The Universe Within, ISBN 3-902038-14-4

Yoga Pathway of the Divine ISBN 3-901665-21-8

The Path of Love, ISBN 3-902038-07-1

Life and Values, ISBN 3-902038-09-8

Akshara Tattva, ISBN 81-87825-02-2

Nava Durga: The Multiple Forms of the Mother, ISBN 3-901665-28-5

Nectar Drops: Sayings of Paramahamsa Hariharananda,
ISBN 3-901665-01-3

Words of Wisdom: Stories and Parables of Paramahamsa Hariharananda,
ISBN 3-901665-00-5

Krishna Katha, ISBN 1-931733-00-7

A Successful Lifestyle, ISBN 1-931733-03-1

Daily Prayers, ISBN 1-931733-02-3

The Changing Nature of Relationships,
ISBN 3-902038-10-1

Prapanna Gita, ISBN 1-971733-01-5

Daily Reflections, ISBN 3-902038-12-8

Kriya Yoga: Path of Soul Culture, ISBN 81-87825-07-3

Gautama Buddha, ISBN 3-902038-16-0

The Body's Dance, the Soul's Play, ISBN 3-902038-17-9

Jnana Sankalini Tantra, PB ISBN 3-902038-18-7,
HB 3-902038-20-9

Rama Katha, ISBN 3-902038-23-2

The Last Decade, A Loving Recollection,
ISBN 3-902038-24-1

River of Compassion: The Life of Paramahamsa Hariharananda (2nd
Edition) ISBN 3-902038-27-6

The Torah, the Bible and Kriya Yoga: Metaphorical Explanation of the
Torah and the New Testament in the Light of Kriya Yoga (2nd Edition)
ISBN 3-902038-29

Other Books about Paramahamsa Hariharananda

Life and Teachings of Paramahamsa Hariharananda
ISBN 3-902038-30-6

In Memoriam (2nd Edition) ISBN 3-902038-31-4

Ocean of Divine Bliss: The Complete Works of Kriya Yoga Master
Paramahamsa Hariharananda (10 volumes)